# How to Use This Book

## Look for these special features in this book:

**SIDEBARS**, **CHARTS**, **GRAPHS**, and original **MAPS** expand your understanding of what's being discussed—and also make useful sources for classroom reports.

**FAQs** answer common **F**requently **A**sked **Q**uestions about people, places, and things.

**WOW FACTORS** offer "Who knew?" facts to keep you thinking.

**TRAVEL GUIDE** gives you tips on exploring the state—either in person or right from your chair!

**PROJECT ROOM** provides fun ideas for school assignments and incredible research projects. Plus, there's a guide to primary sources—what they are and how to cite them.

Please note: All statistics are as up-to-date as possible at the time of publication.

Consultants: William Loren Katz; Kate Roberts, Senior Exhibit Developer, Minnesota Historical Society History Center; Anthony Runkel, Chief Geologist, Minnesota Geological Survey

Book production by The Design Lab

Library of Congress Cataloging-in-Publication Data
Heinrichs, Ann.
 Minnesota / by Ann Heinrichs.
   p. cm.—(America the beautiful. Third series)
 Includes bibliographical references and index.
 ISBN-13: 978-0-531-18584-1
 ISBN-10: 0-531-18584-2
 1. Minnesota—Juvenile literature. I. Title. II. Series.
 F606.3.H455 2008
 977.6—dc22                              2007028462

1 2 3 4 5 6 7 8 9 10 R 18 17 16 15 14 13 12 11 10 09

AMERICA ★ THE ★ BEAUTIFUL

# Minnesota

BY ANN HEINRICHS

Third Series

Children's Press®
An Imprint of Scholastic Inc.
New York ★ Toronto ★ London ★ Auckland ★ Sydney
Mexico City ★ New Delhi ★ Hong Kong
Danbury, Connecticut

# CONTENTS

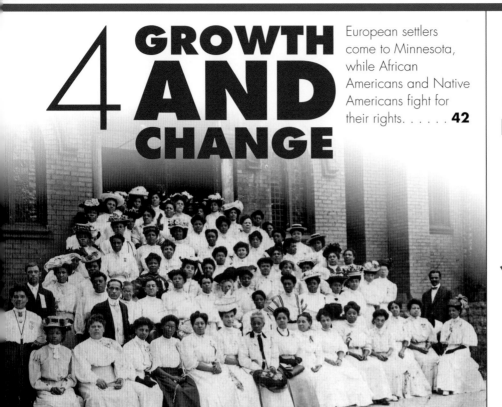

# 4 GROWTH AND CHANGE

# MORE MODERN TIMES

# 9 TRAVEL GUIDE

## PROJECT ROOM

★

BEMIDJI
PAUL BUNYAN
1937

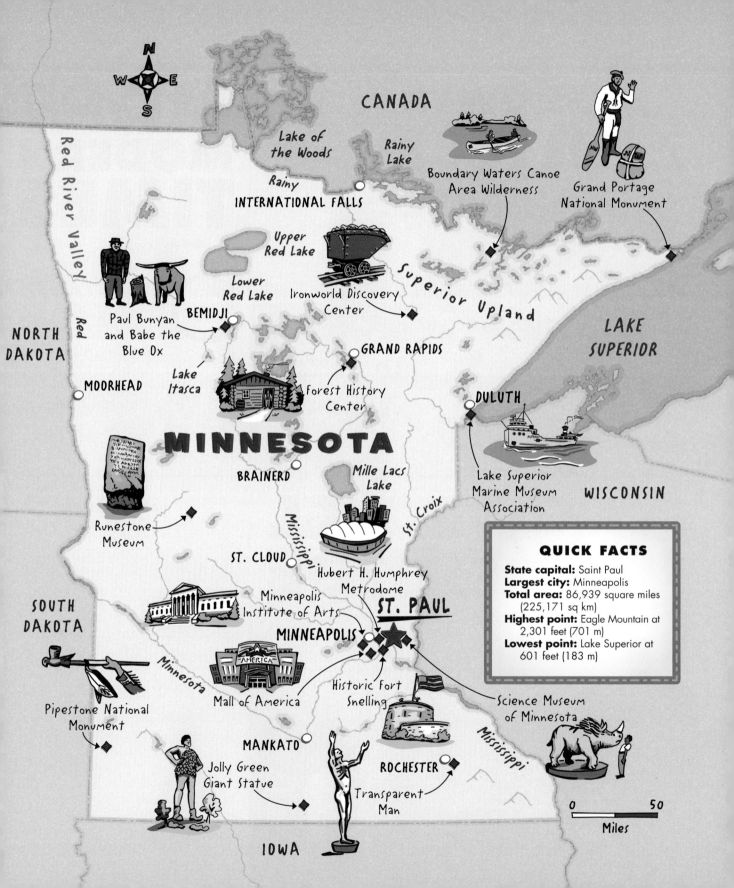

CANADA

N W E S

Red River Valley

Red

Lake of the Woods

Rainy Lake

Rainy

INTERNATIONAL FALLS

Boundary Waters Canoe Area Wilderness

Grand Portage National Monument

Upper Red Lake

Lower Red Lake

Ironworld Discovery Center

Superior Upland

LAKE SUPERIOR

NORTH DAKOTA

Paul Bunyan and Babe the Blue Ox

BEMIDJI

Lake Itasca

GRAND RAPIDS

Forest History Center

DULUTH

Lake Superior Marine Museum Association

WISCONSIN

MOORHEAD

MINNESOTA

BRAINERD

Mille Lacs Lake

St. Croix

Runestone Museum

Mississippi

ST. CLOUD

Hubert H. Humphrey Metrodome

ST. PAUL

SOUTH DAKOTA

Minneapolis Institute of Arts

MINNEAPOLIS

AMERICA

Mall of America

Minnesota

Historic Fort Snelling

Science Museum of Minnesota

**QUICK FACTS**

**State capital:** Saint Paul
**Largest city:** Minneapolis
**Total area:** 86,939 square miles (225,171 sq km)
**Highest point:** Eagle Mountain at 2,301 feet (701 m)
**Lowest point:** Lake Superior at 601 feet (183 m)

Pipestone National Monument

MANKATO

Jolly Green Giant Statue

ROCHESTER

Transparent Man

Mississippi

0       50
Miles

IOWA

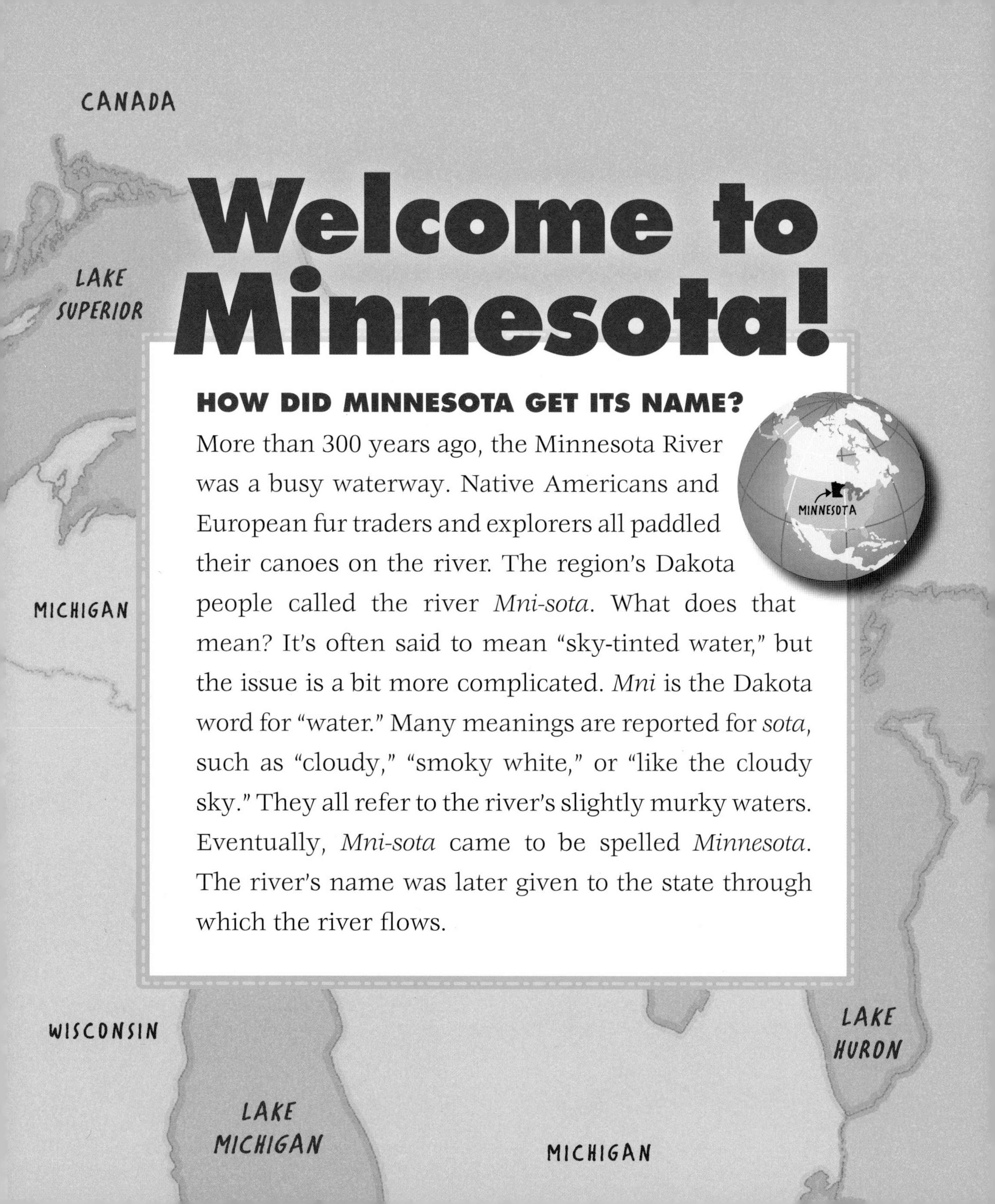

CANADA

LAKE SUPERIOR

# Welcome to Minnesota!

## HOW DID MINNESOTA GET ITS NAME?

More than 300 years ago, the Minnesota River was a busy waterway. Native Americans and European fur traders and explorers all paddled their canoes on the river. The region's Dakota people called the river *Mni-sota*. What does that mean? It's often said to mean "sky-tinted water," but the issue is a bit more complicated. *Mni* is the Dakota word for "water." Many meanings are reported for *sota*, such as "cloudy," "smoky white," or "like the cloudy sky." They all refer to the river's slightly murky waters. Eventually, *Mni-sota* came to be spelled *Minnesota*. The river's name was later given to the state through which the river flows.

MINNESOTA

MICHIGAN

WISCONSIN

LAKE HURON

LAKE MICHIGAN

MICHIGAN

8

## READ ABOUT

Split Rock Lighthouse on Lake Superior

LAND LAND LAND LAND LAND LAND

CHAPTER ONE

# LAND

★

LOOK OUT FROM THE TOP OF EAGLE MOUNTAIN, AND YOU'LL SEE WHY MINNESOTA IS CALLED THE LAND OF 10,000 LAKES. Nestled amid the wilderness far below are many sparkling lakes. This peak, at 2,301 feet (701 meters), is Minnesota's highest point. It's just a few miles from the state's lowest point, Lake Superior, which is 601 feet (183 m) above sea level. On a clear day, you can see Lake Superior from Eagle Mountain. Minnesota spreads across 86,939 square miles (225,171 square kilometers). Within its borders are deep forests, rushing rivers, rolling plains—and quite a few more than 10,000 lakes!

The landscape of Voyageurs National Park was sculpted by glaciers thousands of years ago.

## WORD TO KNOW

**glaciers** *slow-moving masses of ice*

## WHERE IS MINNESOTA?

Look at a map of the United States and you'll see that Minnesota is in the far north. East to west, it looks like Minnesota is just to the east of center. North of Minnesota you'll find Canada. To the west are North Dakota and South Dakota. Iowa lies to the south. To the east are Wisconsin and Lake Superior, one of North America's Great Lakes.

## LAND REGIONS

Massive sheets of ice called **glaciers** once covered most of Minnesota. For hundreds of thousands of years, they lurched and shifted across the land—gouging it, scraping it, and leaving debris behind. When the glaciers melted, they left behind a lot of water and sediment, which also

# Minnesota Geo-Facts

Along with the state's geographical highlights, this chart ranks Minnesota's land, water, and total area compared to all other states.

**Total area; rank** . . . . . . .86,939 square miles (225,171 sq km); 12th
**Land; rank** . . . . . . . . . .79,610 square miles (206,189 sq km); 14th
**Water; rank** . . . . . . . . . . . .7,329 square miles (18,982 sq km); 8th
**Inland water; rank** . . . . . . .4,783 square miles (12,388 sq km); 3rd
**Great Lakes; rank** . . . . . . . .2,546 square miles (6,594 sq km); 5th
**Geographic center** . . . . . . . . . . . . . . Crow Wing, 10 miles (16 km)
southwest of Brainerd
**Longitude** . . . . . . . . . . . . . . . . . . . . . . . 89°34′ W to 97°12′ W
**Latitude** . . . . . . . . . . . . . . . . . . . . . . . . 43°34′ N to 49°23′ N
**Highest point** . . . . . . . . . . . Eagle Mountain at 2,301 feet (701 m)
**Lowest point** . . . . . . . . . . . . . . Lake Superior at 601 feet (183 m)
**Largest city** . . . . . . . . . . . . . . . . . . . . . . . . . . . .Minneapolis
**Longest river** . . .Mississippi River, 680 miles (1,094 km) in Minnesota

Source: U.S. Census Bureau

**Rhode Island, the nation's smallest state, would fit inside Minnesota 56 times. St. Louis County, Minnesota's largest county, would hold four Rhode Islands!**

shaped the land. These forces carved Minnesota's four major land regions—the Superior Upland, the Young Drift Plains, the Dissected Till Plains, and the Driftless Area.

## The Superior Upland

The Superior Upland covers parts of northern Minnesota. This is the most rugged part of the state. Beneath the surface is hard rock that is part of the very old core of the North American continent, more than a billion years old. In places, it contains valuable metals such as iron, copper, and nickel. Iron from this region has made Minnesota the nation's top iron producer.

**An autumn view of the Sawtooth Mountains**

Minnesota's northeastern tip is the wildest region of all. Because of its shape, it's often called the Arrowhead Region. To the east, this region borders Lake Superior, which lies along the U.S.-Canada border. Lake Superior is Minnesota's largest, deepest lake. Of the five Great Lakes, it's the biggest of them all. Along Lake Superior are jagged, pointy hills called the Sawtooth Mountains. A few miles inland is Eagle Mountain, the state's highest peak.

Along the northern border is a notch of land called the Northwest Angle. Most of the Northwest Angle consists of Lake of the Woods. In fact, to get to the Angle you'd have to travel through Canada, boat across the lake, or take a plane.

## The Young Drift Plains

The state's largest land region is the Young Drift Plains. The plains spread across much of western, central, and southern Minnesota, and parts of the north. As the glaciers moved across this area, they left behind material called drift. The drift includes till, which is a mixture of clay, sand, and larger rocks. The till became some of the nation's most fertile soil, making this a rich farming region.

However, not all of this region can be farmed. In central Minnesota, glaciers deposited large, stony masses called moraines. This created both hills and lakes.

Lake Agassiz once covered the northern part of the Young Drift Plains. At its maximum, it covered more than 140,000 square miles (362,600 sq km) across what are now northern Minnesota and parts of Canada—an area greater than that of all of today's Great Lakes combined. This gigantic ancient lake formed from melting glaciers. As the water drained out of Lake Agassiz and other glacial lakes, it carved the courses of many of the major rivers in the region, including the Red River valley. The region that was once the bottom of Lake Agassiz is now extremely flat.

Hundreds of lakes still dot the Young Drift Plains, including Leech Lake, Lake Winnibigoshish, and Mille Lacs Lake. The largest lake entirely within Minnesota is Red Lake,

**MINI-BIO**

### SIGURD OLSON: PROTECTING THE WILDERNESS

In 1921, Sigurd Olson (1899–1982) took his first canoe trip in northern Minnesota. He fell in love with the region and worked to make it a protected area. Through his efforts, both the Boundary Waters Canoe Area Wilderness and Voyageurs National Park were established. Olson spent most of his life around Ely, guiding canoe trips and writing about the Boundary Waters area. Today, he is honored as one of the greatest environmentalists of the 20th century.

**? Want to know more?** See www.uwm.edu/Dept/JMC/Olson/profile.htm

## FAQ

### Q: HOW BIG IS A LAKE?

A: For Minnesota, that's a big question. Although it's called the Land of 10,000 Lakes, Minnesota may have between 11,000 and 22,000 lakes. It all depends on how large a body of water has to be before you can call it a true lake! One standard says a lake must cover at least 10 acres (4 hectares). By that measure, Minnesota has 11,842 lakes.

Boaters prepare to set their boat in Lake Itasca.

**Q8 HOW LONG DOES IT TAKE WATER TO GET FROM LAKE ITASCA TO THE GULF OF MEXICO?**

**A8** Let's say a raindrop fell into Lake Itasca. That raindrop would reach the Gulf of Mexico in about 90 days!

in the northwestern part of the state. The lake's name is a translation from the Ojibwe name, which described the way it looked at sunrise and sunset.

Lake Itasca, in north-central Minnesota, is the source of the Mississippi River, one of the world's major waterways. At Lake Itasca, the Mississippi is so narrow and shallow you can easily wade across it. About 2,350 miles (3,780 km) later, the mighty Mississippi River empties into the Gulf of Mexico. It is the longest river in the United States.

The Mississippi's major tributaries, or branches, in Minnesota are the St. Croix River and the Minnesota River. The St. Croix forms much of Minnesota's border with Wisconsin. The Minnesota River rises on the western border and flows all the way across the state. It joins the Mississippi River near Minneapolis, the state's largest city.

# Minnesota Topography

Use the color-coded elevation chart to see on the map Minnesota's high points (orange) and low points (green). Elevation is measured as the distance above or below sea level.

Minnesota's lakes have a total shoreline of more than 90,000 miles (145,000 km). That's more shoreline than California, Hawaii, and Florida combined!

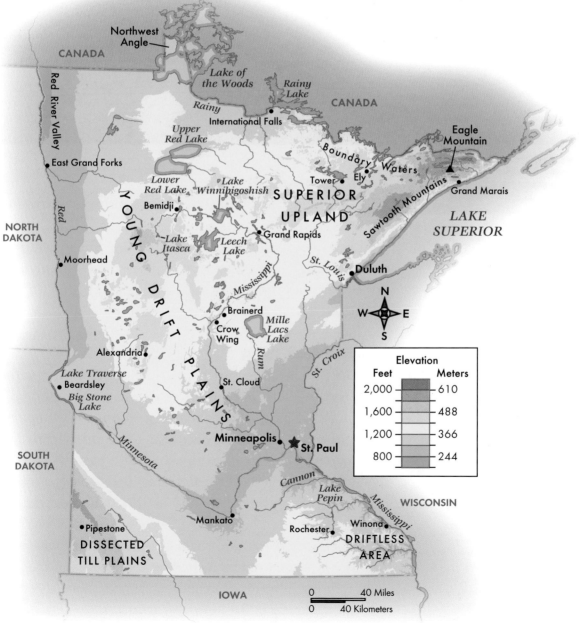

A farmer harvests soybeans in a Minnesota field.

### The Dissected Till Plains

The Dissected Till Plains cover the southwest corner of the state. This region is rougher than the surrounding plains. Here glaciers also deposited till. But in contrast to the Young Drift Plains, this till was later deeply dissected, or cut up, by streams. The level land in the Dissected Till Plains is good for farming.

### The Driftless Area

The Driftless Area is a strip of land along the Mississippi River in the southeast corner of the state. Although glaciers reached parts of southeastern Minnesota long ago, they did not have the impact that the more recent glaciers had on the rest of Minnesota. The western part of the Driftless Area is fairly flat. But in the east, streams cut deep grooves into the land as they rush toward the Mississippi River. These grooves expose layers of rock laid down about 500 million years ago when most of North America was covered by a shallow sea. Fossils of the animals that lived in this sea can be found in these layers.

## MINNESOTA WEATHER

An old joke says that Minnesota has four seasons: almost winter, winter, still winter, and road construction. That last one is summer. That's when the snow and ice are gone, so workers can finally get out and do road repairs.

The joke is an exaggeration, of course, but it's true that Minnesota winters are long and cold. On February 2, 1996, the town of Tower reached the state's coldest temperature ever of –60°F (–51°C). January is usually the coldest month of the year, while July is the hottest. Temperatures begin to drop in October, and the changing leaves are a spectacular sight. Things start to warm up again in late March, and in April and May, flowers begin to brighten the landscape.

## Weather Report

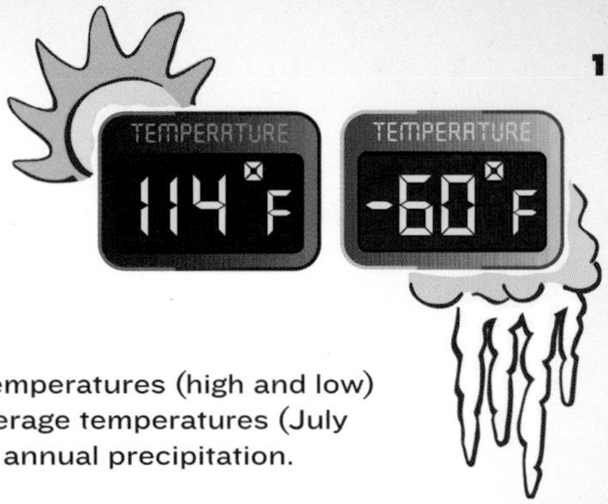

**114°F**

**-60°F**

This chart shows record temperatures (high and low) for the state, as well as average temperatures (July and January) and average annual precipitation.

**Record high temperature** . . . . . . . . . . . 114°F (46°C) at Beardsley on July 29, 1917, and at Moorhead on July 6, 1936
**Record low temperature** . . . . . . . . . . . . . –60°F (–51°C) at Tower on February 2, 1996
**Average July temperature** . . . . . . . . . . . . . . . . . . . . .73°F (23°C)
**Average January temperature** . . . . . . . . . . . . . . . 13°F (–11°C)
**Average yearly precipitation** . . . . . . . . . . . . . 29 inches (74 cm)

Source: National Climatic Data Center, NESDIS, NOAA, U.S. Dept. of Commerce

## WOW

More than 8 miles (13 km) of skyways crisscross downtown Minneapolis. They allow people to walk from one building to the next without having to go outside into the frigid air.

Blizzard conditions in the city of Brainerd

## WORD TO KNOW

**precipitation** *all water that falls to the earth, including rain, sleet, hail, snow, dew, fog, and mist*

During the winter of 1949–1950, Grand Portage State Park in the far northeast got the state's record snowfall for one season—170 inches (432 cm).

# RETURN OF THE WOLVES

The haunting howls of timber wolves (also called gray wolves) once echoed across the United States. But by 1974, they had almost disappeared from every state but Alaska. Only a few hundred wolves remained in Minnesota, and the wolf was considered an endangered species. Wolves were commonly killed because they prey on farm animals. Today, Minnesota has a program that pays for livestock killed by wolves. The International Wolf Center in Ely studies wolf populations and helps them survive by educating the public. In 2007, the timber wolf was removed from the endangered species list in Minnesota.

Most of the state's **precipitation** falls in the eastern areas, while the far northwest gets the least. Western Minnesota gets about 30 inches (76 centimeters) of snow a year, while the northeast can get more than 70 inches (178 cm). In much of the state, snow covers the ground and the lakes are frozen for months on end.

## ANIMAL LIFE

Minnesota's wilderness areas make a great home for black bears, moose, and white-tailed deer. Timber wolves, or gray wolves, roam through the forests, too. Smaller animals found in Minnesota include bobcats, raccoons, beavers, foxes, skunks, muskrats, and otters. Up in the leafy branches, you'll see tree squirrels and even flying squirrels. In forests and tall grasses, there are wild turkeys, ruffed grouse, quail, and pheasants.

Timber wolf

A loon sitting in a nest on a Minnesota lake

You'll probably hear a loon, the state bird, before you see it. This ducklike bird has a wild, weird, cackling call. That's how we got the saying "crazy as a loon"! Loons are common in the northern lakes.

Ducks and geese stop by the lakes to rest and feed during their migrations. Plenty of walleye (the state fish), trout, salmon, muskellunge, bass, pike, and other fish swim in the waters.

## PLANT LIFE

Forests cover about one-third of Minnesota. Pine, spruce, and fir trees thrive in the northern forests. The Norway pine, Minnesota's state tree, can live to be 400 years old! Mixed in among these cone-bearing trees are poplar, aspen, and birch trees. In the southeast, you'll see forests of oak, maple, elm, ash, and walnut. These are deciduous trees, which means they lose their leaves in the fall.

Pinecone

# Minnesota National Park Areas

This map shows some of Minnesota's national parks, monuments, preserves, and other areas protected by the National Park Service.

CANADA

Lake of the Woods

Rainy Lake

CANADA

Rainy

International Falls

Voyageurs NP

East Grand Forks

Upper Red Lake

Lower Red Lake

Ely

Superior National Forest

Grand Portage NM

Chippewa National Forest

Bemidji

Virginia

LAKE SUPERIOR

NORTH DAKOTA

Red

Lake Itasca

Hibbing

Leech Lake

Mississippi

Duluth

Detroit Lakes

North Country NST

Brainerd

North Country NST

Mille Lacs Lake

St. Croix

SOUTH DAKOTA

St. Cloud

WISCONSIN

Saint Croix NSR

0    40 Miles
0    40 Kilometers

Minnesota

Minneapolis ★ St. Paul

Hastings

Mississippi NRRA

Marshall

Mississippi

Mankato

Pipestone NM

Rochester

IOWA

**Legend**

| | National Forest area |
| | National Park area |
| NM | National Monument |
| NP | National Park |
| NRRA | National River and Recreation Area |
| NSR | National Scenic Riverway |
| NST | National Scenic Trail |

N W E S

Blackberries, raspberries, and blueberries grow wild in Minnesota. So does wild rice, which grows in shallow rivers and lakes. In fact, Minnesota has more acres of naturally growing wild rice than any other state. The state's wildflowers include asters, wood lilies, violets, goldenrod, lilies of the valley, and pink and white lady's slippers, the state flower. In the marshy bogs, you'll find insect-eating species such as pitcher plants and sundews.

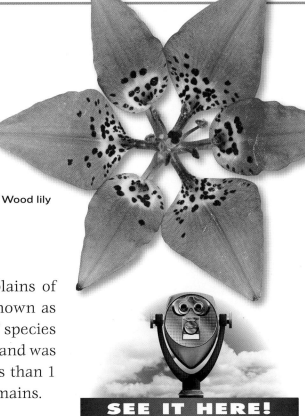

Wood lily

A vast sea of grasses used to cover the plains of southern and western Minnesota. This was known as tallgrass prairie—a community of hundreds of species of grasses, herbs, and wildflowers. Most of this land was cleared and plowed up for farming. Today, less than 1 percent of Minnesota's original prairie land remains.

## PROTECTING THE ENVIRONMENT

Minnesotans love outdoor activities. That's one reason they care so much about their environment. Minnesota has many millions of acres of wildlife preserves and national and state parks and forestlands. The Minnesota Department of Natural Resources oversees the state's natural areas to make sure they are good habitats for animals and plants.

The state's forests are of special concern. Over the years, logging has cleared out much of the state's old-growth forests. Those are forests that have been left undisturbed for more than 120 years. Today, the Chippewa National Forest and the Superior National Forest contain hundreds of thousands of acres of old-growth trees. Wandering in these vast wilderness areas, visitors can experience Minnesota in all its untouched beauty.

### SEE IT HERE!

**THE BOUNDARY WATERS CANOE AREA WILDERNESS**

The Boundary Waters Canoe Area Wilderness is one of the state's most rugged regions. It extends along the Canadian border in northeastern Minnesota, with Voyageurs National Park to the west. This wilderness area covers about 1.3 million acres (526,000 ha) within Superior National Forest. Great glaciers once scraped and gouged this region, leaving jagged cliffs, towering rock formations, canyons, hills, and several thousand lakes and streams. Visitors can hike, camp, or paddle along more than 1,200 miles (1,930 km) of canoe routes.

**22**

## READ ABOUT

Early hunters using stones and spears to fell an ice age mammoth

**c. 8000 BCE**

*Paleo-Indians begin to move into Minnesota*

▲ **c. 3000 BCE**
*People of the Archaic period begin making rock carvings*

**c. 500 BCE**

*Early Woodland people hunt small animals, fish, and gather wild plants*

# CHAPTER TWO

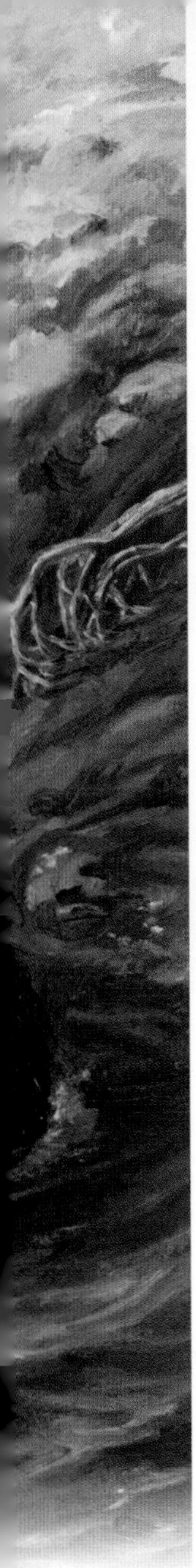

# FIRST PEOPLE

★

**A**S THE REGION'S LAST GLACIER RECEDED, LARGE ANIMALS BEGAN TO ROAM THE LAND. Early humans followed the animals, hunting them for food. Working in groups, they hunted big game such as mammoths, bison, and caribou with stone-pointed weapons. These people, called Paleo-Indians, first ventured into what is now Minnesota around 8000 BCE.

**c. 500 CE**

*People of the late Woodland culture begin harvesting wild rice*

**Late 1600s**

*Ojibwes migrate into Minnesota, pushing the Dakota people south and west*

**c. 1700 ▲**

*Dakotas control the pipestone quarries*

This image of a thunderbird is one of the thousands of ancient carvings found at the Jeffers Petroglyphs Historic Site.

## ARCHAIC, WOODLAND, AND MISSISSIPPIAN CULTURES

A new era began around 3000 BCE. Hunters became more sophisticated, using the powerful atlatl, or spear thrower, to hunt wild animals. They carved elaborate hunting scenes on large stones near the present-day town of Jeffers, in the southwestern part of the state. Over hundreds of years, these **Archaic** people made more than 2,000 rock carvings there. They told their stories through pictures of people, deer, elk, buffalo, turtles, and other figures.

By about 500 BCE, some of the large animals of earlier days had become extinct. Humans adapted by hunting smaller animals in the forests. They caught fish and shellfish in the lakes and rivers and gathered plants for food. **Archaeologists** call them Woodland people. Some of these people made pottery. Some buried their dead in earthen mounds.

## WORDS TO KNOW

**Archaic** *relating to the early, formative phases of a culture*

**archaeologists** *people who study the remains of past human societies*

Around 500 CE, Woodland people of the northern forests began to rely on wild rice for food, in addition to other plants and small game. They harvested rice from the rivers and lakes where it grew. Woodland people in southern Minnesota planted corn. Some built earthen mounds in the shapes of birds and other animals.

In southeastern Minnesota, along the Mississippi River, people built large villages, where they grew corn and other crops. They made pottery. They also made tools out of stone and animal bones. This culture, called the Mississippian, flourished southward all along the Mississippi River. Archaeologists believe that Minnesota's two early cultures—the northern Woodland and the southern Mississippian—evolved into the Dakota people.

## EARLY DAKOTA LIFE

Until the late 1600s, Dakotas were woodland dwellers. They lived in the northern forests, where they survived by hunting, fishing, and doing a little farming. They also harvested the wild rice that grew in the rivers and lakes. Dugout canoes provided river transportation. To make one of these canoes, Dakotas took a log, burned out the center, and hollowed out the burned area for a place to sit.

**FAQ**

**Q8 WHY DO SO MANY PLACE NAMES IN MINNESOTA START WITH MINNE-?**

**A8** Those names come from the Dakota word *mni* ("water"), which is often spelled *minne*. They're all waterways or places near the water. They include Minnehaha Falls; Lakes Minnetonka, Minnewashta, and Minnewaska; and the cities of Minnewawa, Minneiska, Minneota, and Minneapolis!

A Dakota settlement near the Minnesota River

# Native American Peoples

## (Before European Contact)

This map shows the general area of Native American peoples before European settlers arrived.

Ojibwes making a birch-bark canoe

## ENTER THE OJIBWE PEOPLE

In the late 1600s, a new group from the east began migrating to Minnesota. They called themselves Anishinaabeg, although other groups called them Ojibwes (sometimes spelled Ojibwas or Chippewas). Many conflicts broke out between Ojibwes and Dakotas. Ojibwes eventually took over Dakota territory, occupying the forests of northern and eastern Minnesota. The Dakota people moved south and west toward the prairies.

Ojibwes believe that the first man was made when Gitchi Manito, the Great Spirit and creator, blew his breath through a sacred shell onto the four parts of Mother Earth—earth, water, fire, and wind. That created the original man, who was ordered to walk the earth and name all that he saw. Ojibwes believed that all Native American peoples are descendants of this man.

Ojibwes were relying on an ancient **prophecy** when they entered Minnesota. According to the prophecy, they

**The words *chipmunk* and *totem* are derived from the Ojibwe language. *Tepee* comes from the Dakota language.**

## WORD TO KNOW

**prophecy** *a statement or story predicting a future event*

## MAUDE KEGG: ELDER AND STORYTELLER

Growing up among the Ojibwe people of Mille Lacs, Maude Kegg (1904–1996) built wigwams, made maple syrup, collected turtles, and harvested wild rice. She learned to make birch-bark baskets and create designs out of quills and beads. She also listened to stories the elders told. Later, she told her tales to John Nichols, who recorded them in *Portage Lake: Memories of an Ojibwe Childhood.* In 1990, the National Endowment for the Arts gave Kegg a National Heritage Fellowship award in honor of her role in preserving Ojibwe culture.

**?** **Want to know more?** See http://voices.cla.umn. edu/vg/Bios/entries/kegg_maude.html

**WORD TO KNOW**

**breechcloths** *garments worn by men over their lower bodies*

were to migrate west until they found the place where "food grows on water." In northern Minnesota, they found wild rice growing in the rivers. Then they knew that Minnesota was to be their new home.

Besides harvesting wild rice, Ojibwes hunted deer, bear, and moose and caught fish. Ojibwe men went out fishing at night. Holding flaming torches, they drifted slowly down the rivers in birch-bark canoes, and as they spotted fish, they speared them.

Ojibwes lived in dome-shaped wigwams. The frames were long poles bent into a curve, with the ends driven deep into the ground. The frames were covered with bark and woven cattail mats. In the winter, Ojibwes moved to hunting camps in the northern woods. They made snowshoes to walk through the snow and built toboggans, a type of sled, to transport their belongings. Men went out hunting and trapping, while the women dried the meat to preserve it.

In early spring, groups of several families moved to the sugar bush—a grove of sugar maple trees. There they spent several weeks collecting maple sap from the trees and processing it. They made it into maple syrup and maple sugar, which they ate and traded.

Ojibwes turned deerskin into clothes. Women wore dresses, and men wore **breechcloths** and leggings.

Everyone wore moccasins of tough, durable moose hides or deerskin. Ojibwe women created beautiful designs on leather leggings, moccasins, and bags using porcupine quills and beads.

Dakotas lived in cone-shaped tepees made of wooden poles covered with buffalo hides.

## DAKOTA LIFE ON THE PRAIRIES

After the Dakota people arrived on the prairies, they adapted to new ways of life. Dakota men used bows and arrows to hunt bison, or buffalo, for meat and hides. In the winter, the furry hides made warm cloaks and blankets. When bison were not available, men hunted deer, ducks, geese, muskrats, otters, and other small animals. They also brought home eggs, turtles, and fish to eat.

Women built their families' houses. Winter homes were cone-shaped tepees made of wooden poles covered with several buffalo hides sewn together. Summer

Cradleboard

houses were covered with bark, making them cooler inside. In both types of homes, the cooking fire was built in the center, and smoke escaped through a hole in the roof.

Women gathered wood for the fires and tended the gardens. They grew corn, pumpkins, beans, and melons. Dakotas ate these foods raw or boiled, or dried them for future use. Both women and children picked berries and dug *tipsinna*. Sometimes called the Dakota turnip, this sweet, starchy root was ground into flour or made into little cakes. If maple trees grew in the area, members of the Dakota villages tapped them for their sweet sap, which they made into maple syrup and sugar. This, too, was a woman's job.

Dakotas made clothing from the skins of deer, elk, or buffalo. Women decorated clothing with beads, bones, and other objects sewn in intricate designs. Moccasins for the winter were made of buffalo hide with the furry part inside.

Dakotas call the Great Spirit and creator Wakan Tanka, or the Grandfather. Another important Dakota spirit was the White Buffalo Calf Woman. Dakotas believe she presented them with a sacred pipe and seven sacred ceremonies to promote a civilized way of life.

*Picture Yourself . . .*

**Growing Up in a Dakota Camp**

First, picture yourself as a baby. You are carried on a cradleboard—an oak board on which you are laced up in a kind of sack. Your mother carries you in the cradleboard on her back like a backpack. If you are the firstborn girl, you are known as Winona. If you are the firstborn son, your name is Chaska. Later, as you grow up, you will get a special name all your own.

When you are older, in the spring and summer you go out to gather berries, nuts, and roots. You help guard the fields, too. From a wooden platform, you watch for blackbirds that come to eat the corn. When they come, you throw rocks and sticks at them to scare them away. If you are a boy, you have your own child-sized bow and arrow, and you hunt squirrels, rabbits, and other small animals. If you are a girl, you help weed the garden and prepare food for cooking.

There's time for fun, too. You play a game like lacrosse, using a wooden ball and a stick with a net on the end. In the winter, you make a sled out of bark or bison bones and coast down the snowy hillsides. At night, you huddle around the campfire for storytelling. Then, wrapped in your bison robe, you dream of ancient legends and wondrous beasts.

The Indians dug a soft red stone, called pipestone, from rock **quarries** in what is now southwestern Minnesota. They carved the stone into ceremonial pipes. Native Americans came from as far away as the Appalachian Mountains in the east and the Rocky Mountains in the west to meet at this sacred place and to gather stones. By around 1700, the Dakota people controlled the area surrounding the quarry, and therefore, the trade in the red stone.

By this time, Europeans were beginning to venture into the Minnesota wilderness. Change was on the horizon for Minnesota's Native Americans.

## WORD TO KNOW

**quarries** *wide, open holes from which stone or minerals are dug*

### SEE IT HERE!

#### PIPESTONE NATIONAL MONUMENT

Just north of the town of Pipestone are 54 ancient quarries containing catlinite, or pipestone. For centuries, Native Americans traveled here to dig out this fine-grained, red rock. They carved it into sacred peace pipes. Today, the site is protected as Pipestone National Monument. Only people of Native American ancestry are allowed to collect the pipestone. Pipe-making demonstrations are held there in the summer, and visitors may walk the trail around the quarries.

Dakotas at a ceremonial gathering

32

## READ ABOUT

Native Americans
doing business at
a trading post

### c. 1659

*French fur traders Pierre-Esprit Radisson and Médard Chouart, Sieur des Groseilliers, become the first Europeans to reach Minnesota*

### 1679

*Frenchman Daniel Greysolon, Sieur Duluth, reaches the shore of Lake Superior in Minnesota*

### 1680 ▲

*Dakotas capture Father Louis Hennepin and bring him to Minnesota*

## CHAPTER THREE

# EXPLORATION AND SETTLEMENT

★

FRENCHMEN WERE THE EARLIEST EUROPEANS TO TRAVEL THROUGH WHAT IS NOW MINNESOTA. Some hoped to make their fortune. They traded with Native Americans for animal pelts. Others were looking for a water route across the continent all the way to the Pacific Ocean. By the 1600s, the French were already settling in what they called New France, in present-day Canada. Soon the French realized that Minnesota was a rich land worth exploring, too.

◄ **1682**

*René-Robert Cavelier, Sieur de La Salle, claims lands drained by the Mississippi River, including Minnesota, for France*

**1763**

*Great Britain gains eastern Minnesota from France*

**1783**

*Eastern Minnesota becomes part of the United States*

This painting by Frederic Remington depicts explorers Pierre-Esprit Radisson and Médard Chouart, Sieur des Groseilliers, and a group of Native Americans transporting furs on Lake Superior.

## RUNNERS OF THE WOODS

In the 1600s, French fur traders began traveling by canoe into the Canadian wilderness in search of beaver furs. In Europe, beaver-fur hats were fashionable, and there was money to be made in the fur trade. Two traders, Pierre-Esprit Radisson and Médard Chouart, Sieur des Groseilliers, reached today's Minnesota around 1659 while exploring the coast of Lake Superior. This is when Europeans and Dakotas met for the first time.

Radisson and Chouart were *coureurs des bois*, French for "runners of the woods." That was the term for fur traders who didn't have permission from French authorities to trade. In short, they were outlaws. But Dakotas had no reason to care about European law, so they traded with the Frenchmen.

## SIEUR DULUTH

Meanwhile, a French soldier in Canada was hatching an idea—maybe he could find a waterway to the Pacific Ocean. This imagined route, known as the Northwest Passage, inspired many explorers. The Frenchman's name was Daniel Greysolon, Sieur Duluth (sometimes spelled *du Lhut)*. From Canada, he sailed onto Lake Superior, reaching its western shore in 1679. At the time, Ojibwes and Dakotas were fighting over Minnesota. Duluth helped them work out a peace agreement. The agreement didn't last, but Duluth still made his mark on American history. Native Americans told Duluth tales of a great sea to the west. This, he thought, could be the Pacific Ocean!

Duluth continued inland, exploring the St. Croix and St. Louis rivers. He never found the Northwest Passage. Still, as a loyal Frenchman, he claimed the entire region for France. Duluth was the first European to visit the area that's now the city of Duluth, so it was named after him.

Daniel Greysolon, Sieur Duluth, coming ashore

# European Exploration of Minnesota

The colored arrows on this map show the routes taken by explorers between 1654 and 1767.

N
W — E
S

Lake of the Woods

Rainy Lake

Rainy

Grand Mound

Upper Red Lake

Lower Red Lake

Red

Lake Itasca

Leech Lake

St. Louis

LAKE SUPERIOR

Crow Wing

Mississippi

Mille Lacs Lake

Lake Traverse

Chippewa

Rum

Big Stone Lake

St. Anthony (Minneapolis)

Fort Snelling

St. Croix

Minnesota

Des Moines

Mississippi

Radisson and Chouart, 1654, 1660
Daniel Greysolon, Sieur Duluth, 1678–1680
Father Louis Hennepin, 1680
Jonathan Carver, 1766–1767
Fort
Mound
Early settlement
Present-day state of Minnesota

0 — 40 Miles
0 — 40 Kilometers

Father Hennepin visiting Native Americans in a bark-covered home

## FATHER HENNEPIN

Around the same time as Duluth's explorations, King Louis XIV of France sent an explorer named René-Robert Cavelier, Sieur de La Salle, to claim another piece of the North American continent. Father Louis Hennepin, a Catholic **missionary**, accompanied La Salle. In 1680, after reaching today's Illinois, La Salle and Hennepin went separate ways. Hennepin and two other men set out to explore the upper reaches of the Mississippi River. On the way, Dakotas captured them and took them into Minnesota.

When Duluth heard about Hennepin's capture, he met with some Dakotas and convinced them to release the three men. Father Hennepin returned to France and wrote about Minnesota. He had gone on hunting expeditions with Dakotas, and he wrote about the people and the forests. He described a series of waterfalls on

### WORD TO KNOW

**missionary** *a person who tries to convert others to a religion*

The Falls of St. Anthony, the future site of Minneapolis and St. Paul

the Mississippi River that he named the Falls of St. Anthony. In time, the cities of Minneapolis and St. Paul would grow up around these falls. From Hennepin's descriptions, French fur traders soon realized that they should expand their trade into Minnesota.

As for La Salle, he explored the Mississippi River to its mouth at the Gulf of Mexico. In 1682, he claimed all lands drained by the Mississippi for France. That included Minnesota. La Salle named this vast region Louisiana, after King Louis XIV.

## VOYAGEURS

By this time, Canada's French government was issuing permits to fur traders. These fearless wilderness explorers were called voyageurs (French for "travelers"). Some were French Canadians. Others were Métis—people of mixed Indian and French Canadian ancestry. They were

To cover territory quickly, voyageurs paddled their canoes as fast as one paddle stroke per second!

well acquainted with the water routes and the Native people, who actually trapped the animals.

Fur-trading companies hired voyageurs to make trade deals with Indians and to transport supplies and furs to and from trading posts. Explorers hired voyageurs, too, because of their valuable experience.

Voyageur life was exhausting. Often they had to paddle their canoes for 14 hours or more a day. Many voyageurs died by drowning in rapids or storm-tossed lakes. They lived on fish, dried meat, and *rubaboo*—a stew of peas, corn, and animal fat. They also had to carry heavy loads including their canoes over marshy **portages**. Everyone looked forward to the summer rendezvous, or meeting, at a trading post. This was a time for business and for relaxation and storytelling.

## WORD TO KNOW

**portages** *land trails used to carry canoes between rivers and lakes, or around waterfalls and rapids*

### SEE IT HERE!

### THE NORTH WEST COMPANY FUR POST

John Sayer was a partner in the North West Company. In 1804, he built a trading post on the Snake River near present-day Pine City in eastern Minnesota. Sayer traded with the local Ojibwes for wild rice and beaver furs. The post, now a state historic site, has been reconstructed as it looked in Sayer's time. Costumed guides lead visitors around the site and explain how the fur trade worked. The site also includes an Ojibwe encampment.

## *Picture Yourself . . .*

### at a Fur-Trading Post

You live in a log cabin, deep in Minnesota's north woods. Your father works for a fur-trading company. Next to the cabin, he has built another log building as a trading post. Like the Ojibwe children who live nearby, you learn to hunt and to paddle a canoe. Like your father, you learn a bit of the Ojibwe language.

In the trading post, you help your father arrange trade goods on the shelves. There are tin kettles, wool blankets, beads, guns, knives, axes, and other tools. Now and then, Ojibwe hunters come into the post. They carry huge bundles of beaver pelts—skins that have been cleaned and stretched. Your father counts the pelts and then pays the Natives with an array of trade goods.

One day, you hear men singing a hearty French song. Looking out toward the river, you see voyageurs arriving in their canoes. They load up the pelts and head back out toward the trading company's headquarters. The excitement is over until the Ojibwe hunters visit again.

## SEE IT HERE!

### GRAND PORTAGE

Grand Portage, located on Minnesota's northeastern tip, was a footpath around the waterfalls and rapids of the Pigeon River. Ojibwes called it *Kitchi Onigaming*, meaning "great carrying place." At the Grand Portage trading post, on the Minnesota side of the portage trail, Ojibwes traded furs to the voyageurs, and the voyageurs passed them on to Canadian fur merchants. Grand Portage became a center for fur-trade activities and Minnesota's first white settlement. Today, that area is protected as Grand Portage National Monument and is open to visitors.

# THE FRENCH AND INDIAN WAR

Gradually, Ojibwes pushed farther and farther into Minnesota until they encroached on the territory of the Dakota nation. In 1736, Dakotas and Ojibwes went to war. As a result, the Dakota people were forced to move west of the Mississippi River.

Meanwhile, both France and Great Britain were competing for the North American fur trade. This conflict led to the French and Indian War (1754–1763). The Ojibwe nation and other groups to the east aligned themselves with the French. The war dragged on, and by 1760, the British had conquered New France. The war finally ended in 1763 with a British victory. France turned over to Britain most of its land east of the Mississippi River. That included eastern Minnesota.

Minnesota's fur trade was now in the hands of the British. Grand Portage became the fur-trading center for the powerful North West Company. It competed with a

Historic buildings at Grand Portage National Monument

## TRANSLATOR AND FUR TRADER

Pierre Bonga (c. 1780s–?) was an African American fur trader in the Minnesota area. His Ojibwe name was Mukdaweos. Bonga's enslaved parents had arrived in Minnesota with a British officer during the height of the fur trade. They were freed in 1787. Pierre Bonga was educated in Montreal, Quebec, Canada, and then worked for the North West Company and the American Fur Company, often serving as a translator between traders and Ojibwes. He married an Ojibwe woman, and they settled near Duluth. Two of their sons—Stephen and George—became traders, translators, and guides.

rival fur trader, the Hudson's Bay Company. Both companies ran networks of trading posts throughout the region.

## THE REVOLUTION AND THE NORTHWEST TERRITORY

In addition to the land it took in the French and Indian War, Great Britain ruled 13 colonies along North America's Atlantic coast. Britain had been battling France, both in Europe and in North America. To help pay for its wars, Britain charged the American colonists higher and higher taxes. Finally, the colonists couldn't take it anymore. They fought Britain in the Revolutionary War (1775–1783). Their victory led to the formation of the United States of America. All British lands east of the Mississippi River became part of the United States.

In 1787, the new United States set up the Northwest Territory to provide a temporary government for the Great Lakes region. Part of today's Minnesota—the area between the St. Croix and Mississippi rivers—was included in the Northwest Territory.

## READ ABOUT

Dutch immigrants
arriving in
Minnesota,
late 1800s

## 1803

*Western Minnesota
becomes part of the
United States*

## ▲1825

*The U.S. Army completes
Fort St. Anthony,
renaming it Fort Snelling*

## 1851

*Dakotas sign a treaty
giving up their land in
southern and western
Minnesota*

# GROWTH AND CHANGE

★

T RADERS, SOLDIERS, LOGGERS, AND FARMERS FLOCKED TO MINNESOTA IN THE 1800s. Little by little, Native Americans were pushed off their land or persuaded to give it up. Later, immigrants from many lands arrived to build new lives in Minnesota. They helped turn their new home into a top farming, logging, and mining state.

▲ **1858**
*Minnesota becomes the 32nd U.S. state*

**1862**
*Dakotas and settlers fight in the Dakota War*

**1890**
*Iron mining begins in the Mesabi Range*

## THE LOUISIANA PURCHASE

In 1803, France sold its territory west of the Mississippi River to the United States. Because France had named the land *Louisiana*, the deal was called the Louisiana Purchase. Western Minnesota now became part of the United States.

British fur traders were still doing business in Minnesota, however. In 1805, Lieutenant Zebulon Pike was sent to drive them away. Soon the American Fur Company moved in to take their place. French

# Louisiana Purchase

This map shows the area (in yellow) that made up the Louisiana Purchase and the present-day state of Minnesota (in orange).

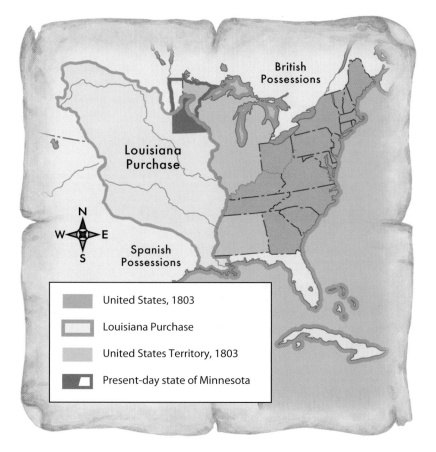

fur traders had been the first non-Indians to explore Minnesota. Now, American fur traders advanced into the wilderness.

Pike had acquired a piece of land from Dakotas. It lay at the point where the Mississippi and Minnesota rivers meet. The U.S. Army built a massive fort there, finishing it in 1825. It was first called Fort St. Anthony, but it was later renamed Fort Snelling. The state's first school was a little schoolhouse at the fort. It opened in the 1820s, teaching soldiers' children and even some of the younger soldiers. The soldiers also built a sawmill and a **gristmill** near the Falls of St. Anthony. This was the beginning of the water-powered industries that would build Minneapolis into a big city.

## WORD TO KNOW

**gristmill** *a water-powered mill where grain is ground into flour*

A view of Fort Snelling in 1848

### MINI-BIO

## HENRY ROWE SCHOOLCRAFT: EXPLORING THE MISSISSIPPI

Henry Rowe Schoolcraft (1793–1864) was a geographer, explorer, and expert on Native American cultures. He learned the Ojibwe language from his half-Ojibwe wife. As an Indian agent for the U.S. government, Schoolcraft helped settle disputes and **vaccinate** Indians against smallpox. On an 1832 trip, he asked an Ojibwe named Ozawindib (Yellow Head) to take him to the Mississippi River's source. Ozawindib took him to the lake, which Schoolcraft named Lake Itasca.

**? Want to know more?** See www.schoolcraft.edu/archives/henry_rowe_schoolcraft.asp

### WORD TO KNOW

**vaccinate** *to administer medicine that protects against a particular disease*

## Picture Yourself . . .

### Living in Early St. Paul

It's 1847. You and your family have just moved to St. Paul, a growing town in the wilderness. Your parents send you to Minnesota's first public school. Some local families had gotten together and hired a teacher, Harriet Bishop, from Vermont. The school is an old log shack that used to be a blacksmith shop. Mud is packed between the logs to keep out the wind and rain. As you study your lessons, Miss Bishop often has to shoo rats and snakes out the door!

## EARLY SETTLEMENTS

For years, Fort Snelling remained the major settlement on the upper Mississippi River. European and American fur traders, explorers, and missionaries lived in the area because the fort provided protection. Many explorers set out from Fort Snelling on their travels. One was Henry Rowe Schoolcraft. In 1832, he followed the upper Mississippi River until he came upon Lake Itasca, the river's source.

Loggers wanted to cut trees in the area between the St. Croix and Mississippi rivers. In 1837, Dakotas and Ojibwes ceded thousands of square miles of this land to the United States. Then settlers and loggers began moving into that area. They founded St. Paul, Stillwater, and St. Anthony (now a suburb of Minneapolis).

Over the years, the area between the St. Croix and the Mississippi had been part of the Northwest, Illinois, Michigan, and Wisconsin territories. Wisconsin

# Minnesota: From Territory to Statehood

## (1836–1858)

This map shows the original Minnesota territory and the area that became the state of Minnesota in 1858.

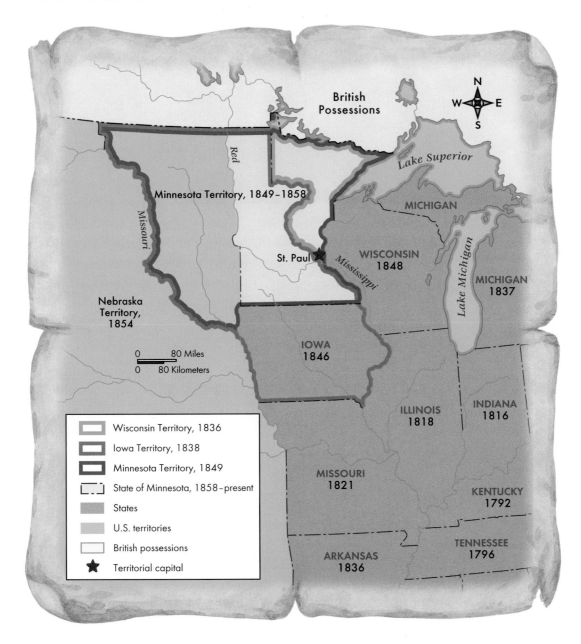

British Possessions

Lake Superior

Red

Missouri

Minnesota Territory, 1849–1858

MICHIGAN

WISCONSIN 1848

MICHIGAN 1837

Lake Michigan

St. Paul

Mississippi

Nebraska Territory, 1854

0    80 Miles
0    80 Kilometers

IOWA 1846

ILLINOIS 1818

INDIANA 1816

MISSOURI 1821

KENTUCKY 1792

TENNESSEE 1796

ARKANSAS 1836

| | |
|---|---|
| ▭ | Wisconsin Territory, 1836 |
| ▭ | Iowa Territory, 1838 |
| ▬ | Minnesota Territory, 1849 |
| ⌐_⌐ | State of Minnesota, 1858–present |
| ▬ | States |
| ▬ | U.S. territories |
| ▭ | British possessions |
| ★ | Territorial capital |

This painting shows the signing of the Treaty of Traverse des Sioux, an 1851 agreement in which the Dakotas gave up all remaining territory in Minnesota.

became a state in 1848, leaving the people in eastern Minnesota with no government. The people met and chose fur trader Henry Sibley to represent them in the U.S. Congress. Sibley urged Congress to create an official Minnesota Territory, and Congress agreed in 1849. St. Paul became the territorial capital.

## MINNESOTA TERRITORY

Minnesota Territory was huge. It was much bigger than today's state. It extended westward all the way to the Missouri River, which runs through today's North and South Dakota. The territory's first **census** in 1849 counted only about 4,600 white settlers. Territorial leaders decided they needed more settlers. There was one problem, though. Most of the farmable land belonged to the Dakota people.

Life was becoming more difficult for Dakotas. As more white settlers arrived and turned the prairie

### WORD TO KNOW

**census** *an official count of the population*

into farmland, bison and other game were starting to disappear. Dakotas began to go hungry. In 1851, they signed a treaty giving up the rest of their land in southern and western Minnesota in exchange for money and food. The treaty covered almost 24 million acres (9.7 million hectares). The Dakota people themselves were confined to two small **reservations** along the Minnesota River.

Tens of thousands of pioneers poured in to farm the Mississippi and Minnesota river valleys. They plowed the prairies and raised corn, wheat, and other crops in the rich soil. By 1857, Minnesota was home to an estimated 150,000 white people.

**MINI-BIO**

## DRED SCOTT: FIGHTING FOR FREEDOM

Dred Scott (1799–1858) had been born into slavery in Virginia. In the 1830s, Scott and his wife, Harriet, were owned by a U.S. Army doctor assigned to Fort Snelling. Before moving there, Scott had lived in Illinois and other territories that did not allow slavery. In 1846, Scott sued for his freedom because he had lived in nonslave territories. The case went all the way to the U.S. Supreme Court. In 1857, the Court ruled that people of African ancestry could not be citizens and thus could not file lawsuits. Though Scott lost the court case, **abolitionists** bought Dred and Harriet Scott, and they were freed the next year.

**?** **Want to know more?** See www.mnhs.org/library/tips/history_topics/99scott.html

## STATEHOOD AND THE CIVIL WAR

Minnesotans wanted to apply for statehood. This wasn't a simple matter, however. At the time, Northern and Southern states were engaged in fierce arguments about slavery. Southern states used enslaved Africans to work their fields without pay. These enslaved people were considered property. But most people in Northern states—and in Minnesota Territory—opposed slavery.

In 1857, the Supreme Court ruled in the Dred Scott decision that people of African ancestry could not become U.S. citizens and that the federal government had no power to ban slavery in territories. This infuriated anti-

### WORDS TO KNOW

**reservations** *lands set aside for Native Americans to live on*

**abolitionists** *people who were opposed to slavery and worked to end it*

slavery members of Congress. The Dred Scott decision sparked a new political party that opposed slavery—the Republican Party—and intensified Americans' arguments over slavery.

Congress sought to keep an even balance between slave and Free States. Finally, on May 11, 1858, Minnesota was admitted as a Free State. It was the 32nd state to join the Union.

The slavery debate was far from over. It finally erupted into the Civil War (1861–1865). Although Minnesota was a brand-new state, it was the first to offer soldiers, including 104 African Americans, to fight on the Union, or Northern, side. Minnesota troops played a critical role in the 1863 Battle of Gettysburg in Pennsylvania.

## NORTH TO FREEDOM

In 1863, Robert Hickman led a great migration of former slaves up the Mississippi River to St. Paul. Hickman had been born into slavery in Missouri in 1831. He learned to read and write and began to preach to other enslaved workers. In May 1863, as news of the **Emancipation Proclamation** began to reach the South, Hickman and dozens of his followers decided to act. They built a large raft, and one night about 75 people boarded it to escape. A steamboat found the raft adrift on the Mississippi near Jefferson, Missouri, and towed it to St. Paul.

Ten days later, another steamship with 218 African American refugees also reached St. Paul, this one escorted by Union troops. They joined the Hickman pilgrims. In 1864, Hickman and his enlarged flock, with aid from local white Baptists, began their own church.

**WORD TO KNOW**

**Emancipation Proclamation**

*an order freeing slaves in the Southern states, issued by President Abraham Lincoln on January 1, 1863*

Robert Hickman

Members of the Pilgrim Baptist Church, which Robert Hickman and his followers founded in St. Paul

With the end of the war in 1865, enslaved African Americans finally gained their freedom. After gaining voting rights in 1868, African Americans in Minnesota worked to advance their other rights. By 1900, St. Paul had the largest percentage of black homeowners of any American city. The city had an educated and strong African American middle class ready to fight for equal treatment.

## THE DAKOTA WAR

The U.S. government had promised the Dakota people payments for land, but payments rarely came. Dakotas were accustomed to hunting and fishing, but their reservations were suitable only for farming, and their crops often failed. They had also been promised food, but they were kept close to starvation. The government traders who ran the reservations' food stores sometimes

## TAOYATEDUTA: DAKOTA LEADER

Taoyateduta (Little Crow) (1810?–1863) was a leader of the Mdewakanton band of Dakotas. In 1858, he led a Dakota delegation to Washington, D.C. They met with President James Buchanan to plead for a fair treaty. Instead, even more land was taken from them. Taoyateduta led his people in the Dakota War. He was shot and killed in 1863 while gathering raspberries in a settler's field.

**? Want to know more?** See www.mnsu.edu/emuseum/history/mncultures/littlecrow.html

cheated Dakotas and refused to sell them any more food. Tensions soon exploded.

In August 1862, Dakotas began attacking white towns. White settlers and U.S. Army troops fought back in what is called the Dakota War. Following six weeks of battles, the Dakota people were defeated. After brief trials, 38 Dakota men were hanged in Mankato, in southern Minnesota, in the largest group execution in U.S. history. Most remaining Dakotas were sent to a reservation in Nebraska.

## IMMIGRANTS

Only about 6,000 people lived in Minnesota in 1850. By 1860, the population had grown to more than 172,000! Where did all those people come from?

Railroad companies wanted more people to settle in Minnesota. More settlers meant more demand for products, which would be shipped by train. So in the 1860s, the railroads began advertising in Europe to attract new immigrants. Brochures promised "wealth and happiness" on Minnesota's "limitless and fertile prairies." The promotions worked. Farmland had become scarce in crowded Europe. So thousands of people from Norway, Sweden, Germany, and other countries packed up their families and came to Minnesota to make a new life farming the rich soil.

Immigrants contributed mightily to Minnesota's agricultural, industrial, and cultural growth. By 1868,

A Red River valley farm, late 1800s

Rochester had a Norwegian newspaper, *Nordiske Folksblad*, that kept newcomers informed about their new home and their old country. The next year, the first Swedish paper appeared. Its aim was to bring more families from Sweden to the United States and make life easier for those who arrived. In 1870, a Swedish American, Hans Mattson, became Minnesota's secretary of state, making him the first Scandinavian elected to high office in the United States.

## BOOMING INDUSTRIES

By 1900, Minnesota's population had grown to more than 1.7 million. At first, farming was the major economic activity in Minnesota. The Red River valley in the western part of the state was the richest wheat-growing region. In the 1880s, many farmers in southern Minnesota began raising dairy cattle.

Hans Mattson

54

## CHARLES A. PILLSBURY: FLOUR INNOVATOR

When Charles Alfred Pillsbury (1842–1899) moved to Minneapolis, he began working in his Uncle John's flour mill. The mill ground wheat into flour using big rocks called millstones. Pillsbury came up with a better way to grind wheat. He introduced steam-powered steel rollers to crush the grain, producing the highly successful Pillsbury's Best flour brand. Large flour mills across the country eventually adopted the steel-roller method. In 1872, Pillsbury founded the C. A. Pillsbury flour-milling company.

**Want to know more?** See http://dromo.info/pillsburybio.htm

## SEE IT HERE!

### MILL CITY MUSEUM

For 50 years, Minneapolis was the flour-milling capital of the world. Water rushing over the Falls of St. Anthony provided the power for dozens of flour mills. At its peak, the Washburn "A" Mill ground enough flour every day to make 12 million loaves of bread! That old mill structure now houses Minneapolis's Mill City Museum. There you can learn about the flour-milling era through hundreds of interactive and hands-on exhibits.

Railroads carried the wheat to flour mills in Minneapolis. There, dozens of water-powered mills ground wheat into flour. Pillsbury and Washburn-Crosby (later called General Mills) were the leading flour mill companies. Minneapolis also had water-powered mills that sawed lumber, wove cloth, and made paper. The city became known as the milling capital of the world. These industries offered even more opportunities to immigrants. Wages were not high, but they were substantially higher than wages for the same work in the immigrants' homelands.

Logging was another thriving Minnesota industry. It started just east of where Minneapolis is today. In time, logging and sawmill activities moved north to the Bemidji area and finally to northeastern Minnesota. Railroads carried logs and lumber down to Minneapolis and out to the prairies. New settlers used the wood to build their homes and barns.

Loggers lived in logging camps for weeks on end. In their spare time, they often told tall tales about the legendary lumberjack Paul Bunyan and his sidekick, Babe the Blue Ox.

## IRON MINING

In the 1880s, Minnesota developed a new industry—iron mining. People from throughout Europe rushed to the mine sites of northern Minnesota for jobs. Miners began digging iron ore from the Soudan Mine in the Vermillion Range in 1884.

Leonidas and Alfred Merritt discovered iron in the Mesabi Range of northeastern Minnesota in 1884, and mining began there in 1890. The Mesabi Range turned out to have vast iron deposits, and by 1904, 111 mines were operating there. Mining began at the Cuyuna Range near Brainerd in 1911. By this time, Minnesota reigned as the nation's leading iron-producing state—a position it still holds today.

In 1914, World War I began in Europe. By 1917, the United States had joined the fighting. Minnesota products were needed in the war effort. The state shipped out millions of tons of wheat, iron, and other goods to be used in making food, weapons, and clothing. By the end of the war, Minnesota's economy was among the strongest in the nation.

## THE LEGEND OF PAUL BUNYAN

The Paul Bunyan legend is believed to have originated among French Canadian loggers. As they sat around the fire in their logging camps, they entertained each other with ever more mind-boggling tales of the gigantic lumberjack and his pet ox: They say that, as a baby, Paul Bunyan ate 40 bowls of porridge at once. Bunyan and Babe the Blue Ox created Minnesota's 10,000 lakes with their footprints. Bunyan used giant mosquitoes to drill holes in trees. He stamped out forest fires with his big feet. Babe could yank roads and rivers until they were straight. On and on the stories went, each more amazing than the last.

Logs ready to haul on an ox-drawn platform, 1890s

## READ ABOUT



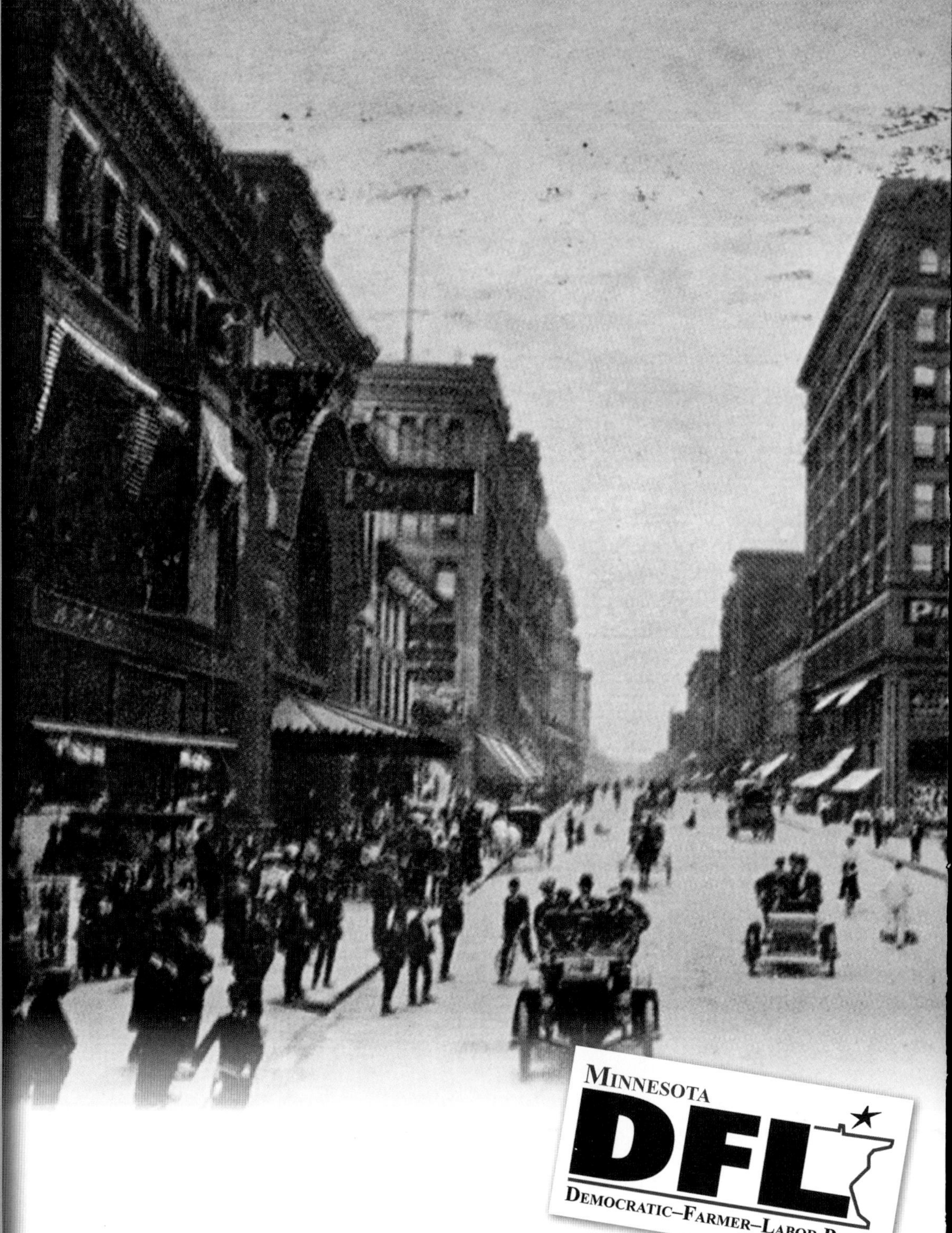

A view of Nicollet Avenue in Minneapolis, 1905

MINNESOTA DFL DEMOCRATIC–FARMER–LABOR PARTY

**1920**
*Racial tensions in Duluth lead to the murders of three African American men*

**1931**
*Four years of drought begin in western Minnesota*

**1944 ▲**
*Minnesota's Democratic Party and Farmer-Labor Party join to form the Democratic-Farmer-Labor Party (DFL)*

# CHAPTER FIVE

# MORE MODERN TIMES

★

A S THE 20TH CENTURY UNFOLDED, MINNESOTANS LIVED THROUGH GOOD TIMES AND BAD. They survived the Great Depression and struggled to gain equality and preserve traditional cultures. Farms became more productive than ever, new industries blossomed, and people moved to the cities. Life was changing quickly in Minnesota.

**1948**

Minnesota senator Hubert Humphrey demands civil rights at the Democratic National Convention

**1977 ▲**

Minnesota senator Walter Mondale begins serving as U.S. vice president

**1999**

The U.S. Supreme Court rules that Ojibwes have the right to hunt, fish, and gather wild rice on their traditional lands

## THE STRUGGLE FOR EQUALITY

Like other states, Minnesota was embroiled in racial tensions in the 20th century. In 1920, a young white girl in Duluth accused three African Americans of assaulting her. Though there was little supporting evidence, the three were thrown in jail. An angry mob of 5,000 people broke into the jail, dragged the three men out, and hanged them from a lamppost. Duluth's black community was horrified. They formed a branch of the National Association for the Advancement of Colored People (NAACP). Then they hired lawyers, who managed to get 21 members of the mob arrested. The next year, Minnesota passed a law against **lynching**. This was just one small step in black Minnesotans' struggle for equality.

## THE GREAT DEPRESSION

Beginning in 1929, the United States was plunged into the Great Depression. Across the country, banks and other businesses closed, and millions of people were out of work. In Minnesota, the statewide unemployment rate reached 29 percent. As many as 70 percent of iron-ore miners lost their jobs. Farmers watched prices for their crops fall. Even worse, a drought struck western Minnesota from 1931 to 1935. Crops withered in the fields.

In 1918, some small-scale farmers, workers, and small-business owners in Minnesota had founded a new political party called the Farmer-Labor Party. They believed that neither the Democratic Party nor the Republican Party did enough to help them. The Farmer-Labor Party reached the height of its power during the Great Depression, when Minnesota's governor, both of its U.S. senators, and most of the state

**WORD TO KNOW**

**lynching** *to kill by mob without a lawful trial*

legislature were all party members. To help workers during these hard times, Governor Floyd Olson, who belonged to the Farmer-Labor Party, signed an order establishing a minimum wage of 45 cents an hour. The Farmer-Labor Party also passed laws lowering taxes and preventing banks from taking away people's homes and land if borrowers could not repay loans.

The U.S. government also brought relief to Minnesotans by sponsoring many employment programs. The Works Progress Administration (WPA) provided jobs building roads, bridges, and parks. The Civilian Conservation Corps (CCC) employed thousands of young men in Minnesota's forests. They planted trees, cut trails, fought forest fires, and built campgrounds.

WPA workers repairing sidewalks in Faribault

## MEAT IN A CAN

In 1937, Austin's Hormel Foods put processed meat in a can and called it SPAM. SPAM sales took off when it became a regular item in the food rations of U.S., British, and Soviet troops. Nikita Khrushchev, the leader of the **Soviet Union**, wrote, "Without SPAM we wouldn't have been able to feed our army." After the war, SPAM became a favorite food of American kids growing up in the 1950s and 1960s.

### WORD TO KNOW

**Soviet Union**  *a former nation in eastern Europe and northern and central Asia; in 1991, it broke apart into 15 smaller countries, including Russia*

During World War II, with many men away at war, women helped keep Minnesota factories running.

# WAR AND POSTWAR PROGRESS

In 1941, Japanese planes dropped bombs on the U.S. naval base at Pearl Harbor, in the Hawaiian Islands. This brought the United States into World War II, which had already been raging in Europe and Asia for two years. The war helped bring Minnesota out of its economic slump. Workers shipped out tons of iron, lumber, and other products to supply the armed forces. Minnesota companies built navy ships and equipment for airplanes and submarines. The U.S. government also built an ammunition factory in Arden Hills called the Twin Cities Ordnance Plant. With men off fighting in the war, women filled many factory jobs.

After the war, Minnesota's industries were stronger than ever. Thanks to new technology, farms became more productive and efficient. Farmers began planting new strains of corn and wheat that resisted disease. New farm machinery made it easier and faster to harvest crops. Hogs and cattle were fattened at automated feedlots, and cows were milked with milking machines.

With all these innovations, fewer farmworkers were needed. Thousands of rural workers moved to the cities to find jobs. By 1950, for the first time, more Minnesotans lived in cities than in rural areas. As the cities swelled, the suburbs grew, because city housing could not hold all the newcomers.

New manufacturing industries developed after the war, too. Control Data Corporation began making computers. New factories also made chemicals and machinery. These companies provided new job opportunities, which was helpful because Minnesota's iron industry

A housing development in Cottage Grove Township, a suburb of St. Paul, which grew from 883 to 4,850 people in the 1950s

**During World War II, 60 percent of the workers at the Twin Cities Ordnance Plant were women.**

took a nosedive in the 1950s. After decades of mining, the state's reserves of high-quality iron ore were dwindling. In time, mining engineers started finding ways to remove taconite, a mineral with low iron content, from rock. Gradually, the mining industry began to bounce back.

## CIVIL RIGHTS AND THE VIETNAM WAR

In 1944, Minnesota's Farmer-Labor Party merged with the Democratic Party to form the Minnesota Democratic-Farmer-Labor Party (DFL). Like the Farmer-Labor Party, the DFL promoted policies that helped average people.

DFL leader Hubert Humphrey was a strong voice for **civil rights** throughout his career. As mayor of Minneapolis in the 1940s, Humphrey barred employers from racial **discrimination** in their hiring practices. At the 1948 Democratic National Convention, he made a dramatic appeal for civil rights, which led the Democratic Party to adopt civil rights as one of its major issues.

In Minnesota, black ministers, community leaders, and newspaper publishers worked for decades to end racial discrimination. But by 1960, many stores, theaters, and other businesses still would not admit blacks. In communities around the state, NAACP members and others took part in demonstrations and other protests. Little by little, doors were opened to African Americans.

Meanwhile, Humphrey, now in the U.S. Senate, worked hard to pass the Civil Rights Act of 1964. It granted African Americans equal rights in employment, voting, and many other areas. Humphrey was elected vice president under President Lyndon Johnson (1965–1969).

### WORDS TO KNOW

**civil rights** *basic rights that are guaranteed to all people under the U.S. Constitution*

**discrimination** *unequal treatment based on race, gender, religion, or other factors*

Members of the NAACP protest segregated lunch counters in St. Paul in 1960.

The Vietnam War also aroused passions in the 1960s and 1970s. The United States had begun sending military advisers to Vietnam in the 1940s, and in 1961 it began sending in combat troops. Many Americans opposed the war. Throughout Minnesota and the nation, college students and others demonstrated against the war. The United States finally withdrew from Vietnam in 1975.

Another leading DFL politician, Senator Walter Mondale, also opposed racial discrimination and the Vietnam War. He was sworn in as President Jimmy Carter's vice president in 1977.

Governor Wendell Anderson signing a proclamation for American Indian Week in Minnesota, 1971

# NATIVE AMERICAN RIGHTS

In the 1950s, the U.S. government began a policy to encourage Native Americans to move off their reservations and into urban areas. Many Native Americans moved to Minneapolis-St. Paul. In 1968, Native Americans in Minneapolis founded the American Indian Movement (AIM) to fight discrimination. The movement soon spread around the country, bringing national attention to Indians' rights.

Minnesota's Ojibwes won a victory in 1999. They had given up their land in 1837 in return for the right to continue hunting, fishing, and gathering wild rice there. But state laws prohibited these activities. In 1999, the U.S. Supreme Court ruled that Ojibwes had the right to carry on their traditional activities on the land they once occupied.

## CARING FOR THE ENVIRONMENT

State officials began paying serious attention to the environment in the 1970s. The state forced iron-ore processing plants to stop polluting Lake Superior with wastes. In the 1990s, hazardous wastes from Minnesota's nuclear power plants became a concern. These wastes released harmful chemicals into the air, soil, and water. Between 1995 and 2000, those chemicals were cut by 23 percent.

Today, the Minnesota Pollution Control Agency has stiff rules governing air and water quality and the disposal of wastes. The agency is constantly testing air, soil, and water in locations throughout the state. Minnesotans are proud of their state's clean environment, and they are committed to preserving it for future generations.

**THINK ABOUT IT!**

# Nuclear Power Plants in Minnesota

Nuclear power generates almost one-fourth of Minnesota's electricity. Supporters of nuclear power say it's a clean, safe, cheap alternative to burning coal. The Prairie Island nuclear power plant near Red Wing is Minnesota's largest nuclear power plant. Radioactive waste, or fuel that has been used up, is stored on the site. The Nuclear Regulatory Commission (NRC), which conducts regular inspections, says the plant is working well and safely. "Overall, Prairie Island Nuclear Generating Plant Units 1 and 2 operated in a manner that preserved public health and safety," said Richard A. Skokowski, an NRC official, after a routine inspection in February 2007.

But many citizens believe the plant poses dangers for the community. The Prairie Island Coalition, a local group opposed to the plant, says, "During normal reactor operations, radioactive substances are routinely produced and released to the environment. These releases are significant. . . . But radiation monitoring is not designed to detect this radioactivity."

# READ ABOUT

A crowd gathers for a charity event at the Target Center in Minneapolis.

CHAPTER SIX

# PEOPLE

★

T HE MANNERS OF MINNESOTANS HAVE OFTEN BEEN DESCRIBED AS "MINNESOTA NICE." That refers to their courtesy and hospitality. Sometimes people say Minnesotans are maddeningly nice—that is, too polite to express an opinion. In fact, Minnesotans do tend to have a friendly outlook. For example, if you are a guest, they may offer you something to eat or drink several times. When you are leaving, they may take a long time to say good-bye. Minnesotans are also generous in donating time and money to charity.

Ice fishing is a popular pastime during Minnesota winters.

## BEING A MINNESOTAN

Minnesotan Garrison Keillor pokes gentle fun at the "Minnesota nice" trait in his public radio show *A Prairie Home Companion*. He also teases about the sober, humble, hardworking lifestyle of Minnesota's Norwegians and Lutherans who live in the fictional town of Lake Wobegon.

On real Minnesota lakes and rivers, ice fishing is a favorite winter pastime. Scandinavians brought this tradition to the area. Fishers cut a hole in the frozen lake, sit on a stool, and catch fish through the hole. Some people drag a little fishing shack out onto the ice so they can fish in comfort. For long fishing trips, shacks might have heaters, beds, and stocks of food!

In contrast, life in Minneapolis moves a bit faster. Residents have access to concerts, theater, comedy shows, and lots of other entertainment. Traffic is heavy in the downtown area, and workers and shoppers bustle among busy offices and department stores. For those who grew up in small towns, it's quite a different way of life! Many big-city Minnesotans welcome the chance to get back to their rural roots. Many city families have lake cabins, and they look forward to spending weekends and summer vacations there.

## WHERE PEOPLE LIVE

About 70 percent of Minnesotans live in or near cities. Minneapolis is the state's largest city, followed by St. Paul, the state capital. Located side by side, these two cities are called the Twin Cities. A whopping 60 percent of all Minnesotans live in the Twin Cities area. Plenty of small towns are scattered throughout the state, though. Northern, far western, and southwestern Minnesota are lightly populated. The little town of Tenney, near the west-central border, registered a population of only six people in the 2000 census. That's a 50 percent increase over its 1990 population of four!

## Big City Life

This list shows the population of Minnesota's biggest cities.

| | |
|---|---|
| **Minneapolis** | 372,833 |
| **St. Paul** | 273,535 |
| **Rochester** | 96,975 |
| **Duluth** | 84,167 |
| **Bloomington** | 80,869 |

Source: U.S. Census Bureau, 2006 estimates

Shoppers and diners outside the Nicollet Mall in Minneapolis

# Where Minnesotans Live

The colors on this map indicate population density throughout the state. The darker the color, the more people live there.

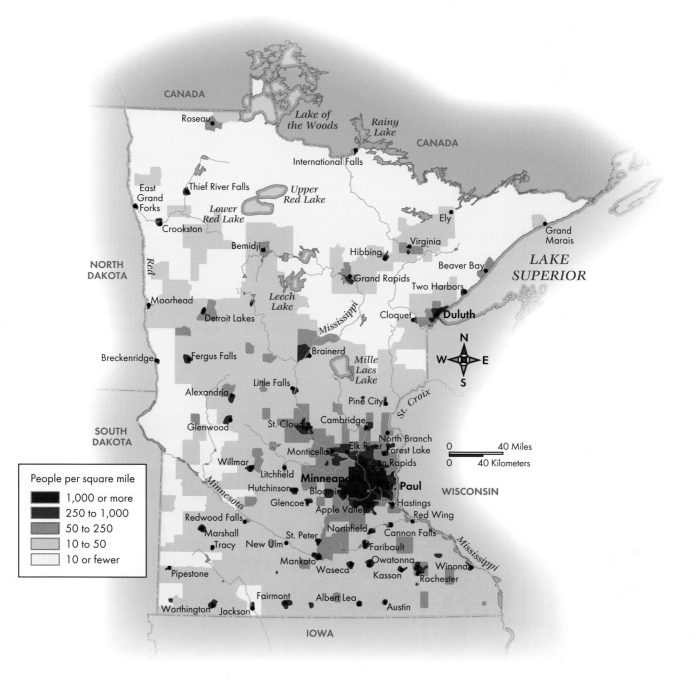

**People per square mile**

- 1,000 or more
- 250 to 1,000
- 50 to 250
- 10 to 50
- 10 or fewer

CANADA

Roseau

*Lake of the Woods*

*Rainy Lake*

CANADA

International Falls

East Grand Forks

Thief River Falls

*Upper Red Lake*

*Lower Red Lake*

Ely

Crookston

Bemidji

Virginia

*Grand Marais*

Hibbing

*LAKE SUPERIOR*

NORTH DAKOTA

*Red*

Grand Rapids

Beaver Bay

Two Harbors

Moorhead

*Leech Lake*

*Mississippi*

Cloquet

Duluth

Detroit Lakes

Breckenridge

Fergus Falls

Brainerd

*Mille Lacs Lake*

N
W E
S

Little Falls

Alexandria

*St. Croix*

Pine City

Glenwood

SOUTH DAKOTA

Cambridge

St. Cloud

North Branch

0    40 Miles
0    40 Kilometers

Willmar

Monticello

Elk River  Forest Lake

Coon Rapids

*Minnesota*

Litchfield

Minneapolis

Hutchinson

Bloomington

St. Paul

WISCONSIN

Glencoe

Apple Valley

Hastings

Red Wing

Redwood Falls

Northfield

Cannon Falls

Marshall

St. Peter

Tracy

New Ulm

Faribault

*Mississippi*

Mankato

Owatonna

Winona

Waseca

Kasson

Rochester

Pipestone

Fairmont

Albert Lea

Austin

Worthington   Jackson

IOWA

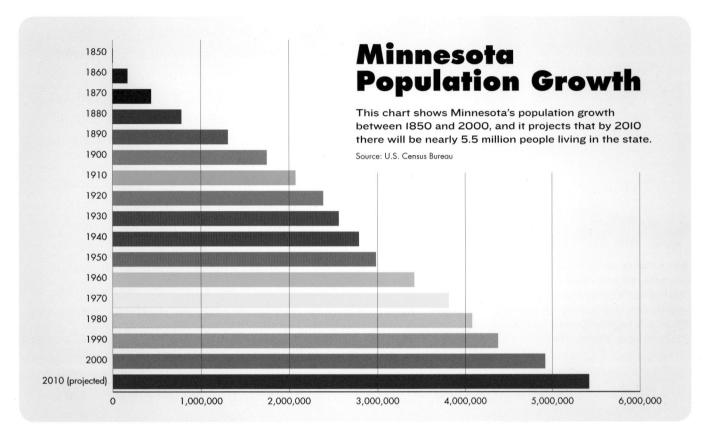

# Minnesota Population Growth

This chart shows Minnesota's population growth between 1850 and 2000, and it projects that by 2010 there will be nearly 5.5 million people living in the state.

Source: U.S. Census Bureau

## ETHNIC MINNESOTA

Minnesotans' ancestors come from all over the world. More than four-fifths of the state's people are descended from western Europeans. Of those, the largest group is made up of people with German heritage. The next most common ancestries throughout the state are Norwegian, Irish, and Swedish.

One after the other, new waves of immigration brought a rich variety of European cultures to the state. Among the settlers were people from Finland, Denmark, Austria, Poland, Russia, Ukraine, Italy, Slovakia, Croatia, Serbia, and Bohemia (now part of the Czech Republic). Many French Canadians settled in the north, near the Canadian border.

Today, immigrants in Minnesota are more likely to be Latino or Asian. Many Latino immigrants came from Mexico, Colombia, and Ecuador. Latinos have lived in Minnesota since the 1860s, and the majority of Latino Minnesotans were born in the United States. In 2004, 175,000 Latinos lived in Minnesota, more than triple the number in 1990.

In the mid-1970s, warfare drove many Southeast Asians out of their homelands. Many of those who found a new life in Minnesota were Vietnamese, Laotian, and Cambodian people. People have also arrived in Minnesota from China, India, the Philippines, and various Middle Eastern and African countries. Many came for better job opportunities. Others, such as immigrants from Somalia, a country in eastern Africa, are political refugees. They established the Confederation of Somali Community in Minnesota (CSCM) to preserve Somali culture and help Somalis become a part of American society.

Most of the state's African Americans live in the Twin Cities area. And many Native Americans live in the Twin Cities as well. Ojibwes and Dakotas are the major Native American groups in Minnesota. There are several Ojibwe reservations in northern Minnesota, while the Dakota reservations are in the south.

**According to the 2000 census, 13 percent of Minnesota's foreign-born residents were from Africa. That's a higher percentage than in any other state.**

# People QuickFacts

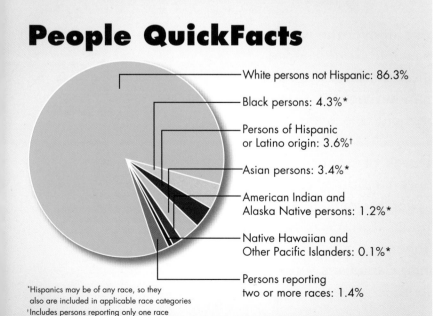

White persons not Hispanic: 86.3%

Black persons: 4.3%*

Persons of Hispanic or Latino origin: 3.6%†

Asian persons: 3.4%*

American Indian and Alaska Native persons: 1.2%*

Native Hawaiian and Other Pacific Islanders: 0.1%*

Persons reporting two or more races: 1.4%

*Hispanics may be of any race, so they also are included in applicable race categories
†Includes persons reporting only one race
Source: U.S. Census Bureau, 2005 estimate

Students work on a class project in Golden Valley.

## EDUCATION

Minnesota residents are the best-educated people in the country, with a higher percentage of high school graduates than any other state. Kids in Minnesota are required to attend school from ages 7 to 16. Most attend public schools, but about 11 percent attend private schools.

Minnesota has dozens of colleges and universities. The largest is the University of Minnesota, with campuses in Minneapolis-St. Paul, Duluth, Morris, Crookston, and Rochester. The state also has many private colleges and universities. St. Paul's Hamline University was Minnesota's first college. Carleton College in Northfield is one of the top small colleges in the country.

## FAQ

**Q8** BESIDES ENGLISH, WHICH LANGUAGES ARE MOST COMMONLY SPOKEN IN MINNESOTA?

**A8** About 9 percent of Minnesotans speak a language other than English at home. The most common of these languages is Spanish. Next are the Southeast Asian languages Miao and Hmong. They are followed by German, various African languages, Vietnamese, French dialects, Scandinavian languages, Chinese, Russian, and Laotian.

## HOW TO TALK LIKE A MINNESOTAN

Minnesotans share some speaking quirks with other people in the upper Midwest. Because of Scandinavian influences, they also have some unique expressions. Here are some common Minnesotan words and phrases:

- come with—used without an object ("Want to come with?")
- leave it go—let it be or don't bother with it
- oh ya, ya sure, you betcha—expressions of agreement
- then—often added to the end of a statement or question ("How's your new dog then?")
- uff da (pronounced *oof dah*)—Norwegian term used to express surprise, exhaustion, disappointment, or dismay

## HOW TO EAT LIKE A MINNESOTAN

Naturally, in the Land of 10,000 Lakes, fish is a popular dish. Walleye is a favorite, and people love to catch their own and cook it. The Friday night fish fry is a summertime event in some communities. Townspeople gather to enjoy fried cod and potato salad. Then there's the traditional Scandinavian lutefisk. This is a special cod dish—and you either love it or hate it!

A flatbread called *lefse* is another Scandinavian favorite. Minnesotans also enjoy pasties—a kind of potpie with meat, potatoes, and vegetables inside. Wild rice and blueberries grow in Minnesota, and they often turn up on the dinner table.

If you drop by the Minnesota State Fair, you'll be amazed at how many foods you can get on a stick. Year after year, vendors try to outdo one another with wild stick offerings. In 2006, someone counted a total of 59 foods sold on a stick. They included deep-fried Twinkies, alligator, cheesecake, pizza—and even spaghetti!

Fried fish

# MENU

## WHAT'S ON THE MENU IN MINNESOTA?

★ ★ ★

## Lutefisk

That's Norwegian for "lye fish." It's dried cod soaked in lye, a chemical solution that draws out the salt. Scandinavians have been eating lutefisk for centuries. They used to make the lye from birch ashes. According to legend, even the Vikings ate lutefisk. The Christmas season is a traditional time for serving lutefisk.

## Potato Lefse

This Scandinavian treat is a flatbread made with riced or mashed potatoes. Sometimes it's wrapped around foods like a bun. Sometimes it's served open-faced, with various foods piled on top. It might be served with jelly, butter, sugar, or syrup. Potato lefse is a traditional food at Thanksgiving and Christmastime. In 1983, people in Starbuck made the world's largest lefse. It measured 9 feet 8 inches (3 m) across!

## Wild Rice

Wild rice was a staple food for Minnesota's Ojibwe and Dakota people. It's an aquatic grass, and Indians harvested it from the rivers and lakes. Some Minnesotans still harvest it by hand from canoes. Today, it's used as stuffing, made into pudding, or served with casseroles. Wild rice is Minnesota's official state grain.

Wild rice

## TRY THIS RECIPE
## Blueberry Muffins

Blueberries grow wild in Minnesota's northeastern bogs and forests. It's no surprise then, that blueberry muffins are the official state muffin. They're easy to make, too! (Be sure to have an adult nearby to help.)

### Ingredients:
½ cup butter or margarine
1¼ cups sugar
2 eggs
2 cups flour
2 teaspoons baking powder
½ teaspoon salt
½ cup milk
1 teaspoon vanilla
2 cups fresh or frozen blueberries

Blueberry muffin

### Instructions:
1. Preheat oven to 375°F.
2. Grease a muffin pan with a bit of butter or put paper liners in the muffin cups.
3. In a large bowl, beat the butter or margarine and sugar. Then add the eggs one at a time, beating well after each one.
4. In a separate bowl, sift together the flour, baking powder, and salt.
5. Add this to the first mixture, alternating with the milk.
6. Blend in the vanilla.
7. Gently fold in the blueberries.
8. Pour the batter into the muffin cups and bake for 25 to 30 minutes.
9. Let the muffins cool in the pan for about 30 minutes before removing.

Makes 6 to 12 muffins, depending on the size of the muffin cups.

Prudence Johnson joins Garrison Keillor for a duet during a dress rehearsal at the Fitzgerald Theater.

## THEATER, MUSIC, AND DANCE

Minneapolis presents an array of theater, dance, puppetry, storytelling, and other performing arts at its Fringe Festival every August. The acts come from around the country, but Minnesotans also enjoy excellent homegrown talent throughout the year.

The Minnesota Dance Theater in Minneapolis has programs and classes for both adults and children. Producer and director Lou Bellamy founded the Penumbra Theatre Company in St. Paul in 1976. It features African American dramas such as those by playwright August Wilson. Minneapolis's Guthrie Theater has been presenting plays for more than 40 years. The Guthrie opened its new three-theater complex in 2006. Garrison Keillor's *A Prairie Home Companion* radio show usually broadcasts from St. Paul's Fitzgerald Theater.

Minnesota-born TV and movie actors include Winona Ryder, Kevin Sorbo, Richard Dean Anderson, Steve Zahn, and Jessica Biel. The TV show *Mystery Science Theater* originated in Minneapolis, too.

Musicians from Minnesota range from the Andrews Sisters and Judy Garland of the 1940s to singer and songwriter Bob Dylan to the funk, rock, and soul star Prince. Dylan's songs, full of political and social commentary, added fuel to the civil rights and antiwar movements of the 1960s. Music legend Prince and the rapper P.O.S. (Stefon Alexander) both started out in Minneapolis.

## MINI-BIO

### AUGUST WILSON: PRIZE-WINNING PLAYWRIGHT

August Wilson (1945–2005) grew up in the Hill District, an African American neighborhood of Pittsburgh, Pennsylvania. When he became a playwright, the Hill District was the setting for his best-known work, a set of 10 plays called the Pittsburgh Cycle. Two of those plays, *Fences* and *The Piano Lesson*, won the Pulitzer Prize for Drama. Wilson lived in St. Paul from 1978 to 1990, and many of his plays premiered at the Penumbra Theatre there.

**? Want to know more?** See www.tcg.org/publications/augustwilson/index.cfm

Minnesota native Bob Dylan performing in Stockholm, Sweden, in 1966

## FRANCES DENSMORE: SAVING THE SONGS

As a child in Red Wing, Frances Densmore (1867–1957) went to sleep every night to the sound of drumbeats from the Dakota camp nearby. Later, as a music teacher, she became interested in Native American music. In the early 1900s, she began visiting Dakotas, Ojibwes, and many other groups. She recorded their songs and sent the recordings to the Smithsonian Institution in Washington, D.C., helping preserve the music and bring it to a wider audience.

**? Want to know more?** See www.mnsu.edu/emuseum/information/biography/abcde/densmore_frances.html

Scandinavian festivals are good places to enjoy folk music traditions. At the Scandinavian Folk Music Festival in Nisswa or the Scandinavian Hjemkomst Festival in Moorhead, you might hear the lively music of the hardanger fiddle, a traditional Norwegian instrument. Covered with decorative designs, it's similar to a violin, with extra strings to provide an echo effect.

Native Americans in Minnesota hold powwows throughout the year. These are religious and social gatherings that bring together relatives and friends. The festivities begin with a grand entry march, when all the participants parade by. Then honored drummers beat out rhythms, while brilliantly costumed dancers compete in traditional dances. Ojibwes hold the White Earth Powwow every June in White Earth. About 500 men, women, and children compete in dances. The Dakota Mahkato Mdewakanton Wacipi is held in Mankato in September.

## ARTISTS AND CRAFTSPEOPLE

Many Minnesotans continue folk arts and crafts traditions handed down from their ancestors. One example is acanthus carving, a Scandinavian wood-carving style. Craftspeople carve designs of acanthus leaves in a graceful, decorative pattern. These designs might adorn shelves, breadboards, candleholders, and other house-

Sculptor James Earle Fraser in his studio, early 1900s

hold objects. Birch-bark boxes are another Scandinavian craft. They're made of curved strips of birch bark, with no nails holding them together. Rosemaling is a traditional Norwegian style of painting flowers, leaves, and scrolls. It's used to decorate cabinets, chairs, and wooden tableware.

George Morrison, born on the Grand Portage Indian Reservation near Grand Marais, was a sculptor and painter. He experimented with abstract and modern styles and became known as both an American artist and a Native American artist. James Earle Fraser, born in Winona, was a sculptor who portrayed Native American subjects. One of his best known works is a sculpture called *End of the Trail*.

An example of rosemaling

## WRITERS AND ILLUSTRATORS

The triumphs and tragedies of pioneer life in Minnesota make good subjects for books. In *Giants in the Earth: A Saga of the Prairie* (1927), Norwegian immigrant Ole

MINI-BIO

## LAURA INGALLS WILDER: LITTLE HOUSE IN MINNESOTA

When Laura Ingalls Wilder (1867–1957) was seven, she and her family moved to Walnut Grove, Minnesota, where they lived in a sod house. It was just a hollow dug into the side of a hill. When she grew up, she wrote about her time there in *On the Banks of Plum Creek*. In the 1970s, Wilder's stories about her pioneer family were turned into the popular TV series *Little House on the Prairie*. Her books are classic stories of life on the frontier.

**?** **Want to know more?** See www.wisconsinhistory. org/topics/wilder/index.asp

Rolvaag wrote about the Norwegian immigrant experience of settling as farmers in America. Children's author Laura Ingalls Wilder and her family were pioneers in Minnesota, too. She wrote *On the Banks of Plum Creek* about their time there.

In the 1920s, Sinclair Lewis wrote about small-town life and working-class people in novels such as *Babbitt* and *Elmer Gantry*. His novel *Main Street* takes place in a town much like his hometown of Sauk Centre. In 1930, he became the first American to win a Nobel Prize for Literature. F. Scott Fitzgerald wrote about life in the Jazz Age of the 1920s. He began his writing career in his hometown of St. Paul.

**Sinclair Lewis working at his typewriter in 1944**

## MINI-BIO

### WANDA GÁG: DRAW TO LIVE, LIVE TO DRAW

When artist Wanda Gág (1893–1946) was 17, she wrote in her diary: "My Own Motto— Draw to Live and Live to Draw." She was born in New Ulm. Her father died when she was 14, and her mother was also sick. To help raise her six younger siblings, she worked at various odd jobs, including illustrating magazine articles and greeting cards. Gág eventually became a children's book writer and illustrator. Children today still enjoy her delightful, expressive drawings in books such as *Millions of Cats*, *The ABC Bunny*, and *Nothing at All*.

**? Want to know more?** See http://people.mnhs.org/authors/biog_detail.cfm?PersonID=Gag173

Artist Mary GrandPré at work on illustrations for
*Harry Potter and the Half-Blood Prince*

Many Minnesotans have written books for young people. Writer and illustrator Wanda Gág published her beloved children's book *Millions of Cats* in 1928. Kids today are familiar with artist Mary GrandPré, though they may not realize it. GrandPré, who attended the Minneapolis College of Art and Design, illustrated the U.S. editions of the Harry Potter books. Kate DiCamillo's

## CHARLES SCHULZ: SPARKY CREATES *PEANUTS*

Charles Schulz (1922–2000) was born in Minneapolis and grew up in St. Paul. He loved comic strips from the time he was a child, and he always wanted to be a cartoonist. His popular comic strip *Peanuts*, with its beloved characters Charlie Brown, Lucy, and Snoopy, first appeared in 1950. *Peanuts* was revolutionary in the world of comic strips. The drawings were simple, and the emotions of the young characters were honest and often quite sad. Schulz, nicknamed Sparky, drew *Peanuts* for almost 50 years. It is one of the most widely read comics of all time.

**? Want to know more?** See www.pbs.org/wnet/ americanmasters/database/schulz_c.html

popular young-adult novels include *Because of Winn-Dixie, The Tiger Rising, The Tale of Despereaux,* and the Mercy Watson series. Other kids' book authors from Minnesota include Gary Paulsen, Mary Casanova, and Marsha Qualey. Then there's the beloved Minneapolis native Charles Schulz. He created the *Peanuts* comic strip.

## SPORTS

Are you going to a Minnesota Vikings football game? Then you'd better put on your Helga Hat! This horned hat with blond braids is a trademark of Vikings fans. The Vikings, in their distinctive purple uniforms, have provided their fans with many exciting moments. With a powerful defensive line nicknamed the Purple People Eaters, the team made it to the Super Bowl four times in the 1970s. The Vikings lost all four times, but many of its star players are still the stuff of legends, including Pro Football Hall of Famer Fran Tarkenton.

Want to see the "Twinkies"? That's what fans sometimes call their professional baseball team, the Minnesota Twins. The Twins are named after the Twin Cities, Minneapolis and St. Paul. The Twins won the World Series in 1987 and 1991.

Basketball fans in Minnesota root for the Timberwolves of the National Basketball Association and the Lynx of the Women's National Basketball Association,

Enthusiastic Minnesota Twins fans

while hockey fans cheer for the Minnesota Wild. Many hockey fans make their way to Eveleth, home to the United States Hockey Hall of Fame.

Many Minnesotans enjoy ice-skating, hockey, skiing, bobsledding, snowmobiling, and snowshoeing in winter. Broomball and curling are favorites, too. Broomball is a bit like ice hockey. Players hit a ball toward the net with their "broom"—a stick with a triangular head. Curling involves sliding a heavy granite stone across the ice. The men's and women's U.S. Olympic curling teams are based in Bemidji, and Olympic competitors and sisters Cassie and Jamie Johnson were raised there.

Minnesotans' love of the outdoors means they get out and get lots of exercise. In 2006, almost 86 percent of Minnesotans took part in regular physical activities. That's the highest rate in the country. Not surprisingly, Minnesotans live longer than people in any other state except Hawai'i. The Land of 10,000 Lakes keeps its people in good shape.

## SEE IT HERE!

**MINNEAPOLIS AQUATENNIAL**

In the summer, many Minnesotans enjoy boating, swimming, and water-skiing. But the Minneapolis Aqua-tennial features more unusual sports. This popular summertime festival has been held every July since 1940. It includes a sand-castle building contest and a race for boats made entirely of milk cartons. When racing milk-carton boats, creativity is more important than speed.

84

## READ ABOUT

Students touring the Minnesota state capitol in St. Paul

# CHAPTER SEVEN

# GOVERNMENT

★

**F**IFTH GRADERS FROM BAYPORT DECIDED TO GET INVOLVED IN GOVERNMENT. They knew that Minnesota had no state fruit. But scientists at the University of Minnesota had developed a crisp, juicy apple called the Honeycrisp. Farmers were growing it all over the world. So in 2006, the students gave speeches before their state lawmakers about the Honeycrisp. They were nervous, but they made a convincing case. The lawmakers voted to make the Honeycrisp the official state fruit. The governor even signed the law at the kids' school!

## Capitol Facts

Here are some fascinating facts about Minnesota's state capitol.

**Height:** 223 feet (68 m)
**Length:** 434 feet (132 m)
**Width:** 229 feet (70 m)
**Dome diameter (outside):** 89 feet (27 m)
**Dome material:** Marble
**Construction dates:** 1896–1905
**Architect:** Cass Gilbert
**Cost of construction:** $4.5 million

## THE CENTER OF GOVERNMENT

Those Bayport students met with lawmakers in St. Paul, Minnesota's capital city. That's the seat of state government, where the major government activities take place. The main government building is a massive white structure called the state capitol. When the capitol opened in 1905, an architecture critic wrote: "When its white dome first swims into view there is a shock of surprise, then a rapidly growing delight in its pure beauty." That building still stands today, housing Minnesota's three branches of government—the legislative, executive, and judicial branches.

## Capital City

This map shows places of interest in St. Paul, Minnesota's capital city.

The state capitol in St. Paul

## THE LEGISLATIVE BRANCH

Minnesota state lawmakers make up the legislative branch of government. The lawmakers bring up suggestions for new laws, study and discuss them, and vote on them.

Like the U.S. Congress, the state legislature is made up of two houses—the senate and the house of representatives. Voters elect senators and representatives from districts around the state. District boundaries are drawn according to population, so that all citizens are represented equally.

Minnesota's 67 state senators serve four-year terms. Its 134 representatives serve two-year terms. There is one exception to this rule, though. Every 10 years,

### SEE IT HERE!

#### THE STATE CAPITOL

When you're in St. Paul, be sure to visit the state capitol. The architect Cass Gilbert modeled it after St. Peter's Basilica, an enormous church in Rome, Italy. Like St. Peter's, the capitol has a dome made of marble. Only a few buildings in the world have marble domes. Look above the main entrance, and you'll see a golden four-horse chariot glistening in the sun. The sculpture symbolizes Minnesota's progress. Inside the capitol, large paintings of scenes from Minnesota history adorn the walls. You can gaze up into the soaring dome or watch the state lawmakers at work. Outside, look into the distance, and you'll see Minnesota's landscape stretching far beyond the city.

## HUBERT H. HUMPHREY: THE HAPPY WARRIOR

Hubert H. Humphrey (1911–1978) was born in South Dakota and later settled in Minnesota. He was the U.S. vice president under President Lyndon B. Johnson (1965–1969). He also served as a U.S. senator from Minnesota (1949–1964 and 1971–1978). In 1968, he was the Democratic nominee for president, but he lost to Republican Richard Nixon. Humphrey's nickname in the Senate was the Happy Warrior because he fought for social programs that improved ordinary people's lives.

**? Want to know more?** See www.lbjlib.utexas.edu/johnson/archives.hom/FAQs/humphrey/HHH_home.asp

State legislators gather to watch Governor Tim Pawlenty sign the Freedom to Breath act in 2007.

following the U.S. census, the state redraws the boundaries of its legislative districts based on shifts in population. In order to make this transition, senators who were elected in years that end in zero serve two-year terms.

## THE EXECUTIVE BRANCH

The job of the executive branch is to enforce state laws. Minnesota's governor is the head of the executive branch, and his or her office is also in the capitol. The governor and the lieutenant governor are elected together to a four-year term.

# Representing Minnesotans

This list shows the number of elected officials who represent Minnesota, both on the state and national levels.

| OFFICE | NUMBER | LENGTH OF TERM |
| --- | --- | --- |
| **State senators** | 67 | 4 years |
| **State representatives** | 134 | 2 years |
| **U.S. senators** | 2 | 6 years |
| **U.S. representatives** | 8 | 2 years |
| **Presidential electors** | 10 | — |

# Minnesota's State Government

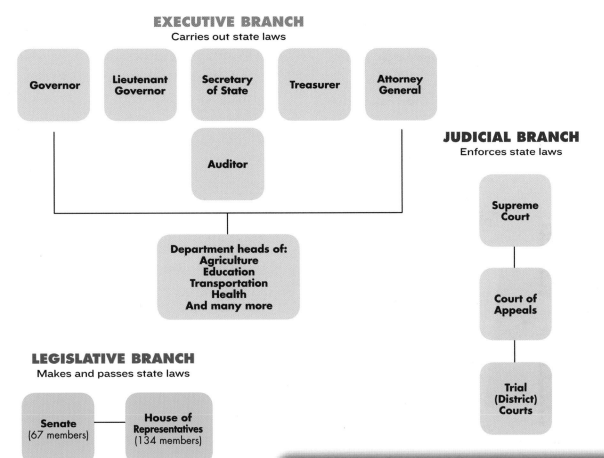

**EXECUTIVE BRANCH**
Carries out state laws

Governor

Lieutenant Governor

Secretary of State

Treasurer

Attorney General

Auditor

Department heads of:
Agriculture
Education
Transportation
Health
And many more

**JUDICIAL BRANCH**
Enforces state laws

Supreme Court

Court of Appeals

Trial (District) Courts

**LEGISLATIVE BRANCH**
Makes and passes state laws

Senate (67 members)

House of Representatives (134 members)

Voters also elect three other executive officers—the secretary of state, the attorney general, and the state auditor. They, too, serve four-year terms. The governor appoints the heads of many departments and commissions. These include offices that oversee agriculture, education, pollution control, transportation, labor, health, and housing.

## WEIRD MINNESOTA LAWS

Like many other states, Minnesota has some strange laws. These are still on the books but are no longer enforced.

- Mosquitoes are officially public nuisances throughout Minnesota.
- No one may cross state lines with a duck on top of his or her head.
- It is illegal to tease skunks.
- All bathtubs must have feet.
- If a woman impersonates Santa Claus, she may face 30 days in jail.
- In Brainerd, every man is required to grow a beard.

Warren Burger of St. Paul joined the U.S. Supreme Court in 1969. Harry Blackmun, who also grew up in St. Paul, joined the Court in 1970. The two, who were close friends in childhood, were often called the Minnesota Twins!

MINI-BIO

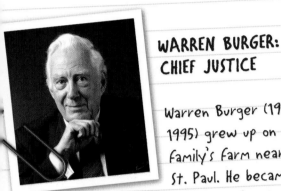

## WARREN BURGER: CHIEF JUSTICE

Warren Burger (1907–1995) grew up on his family's farm near St. Paul. He became a lawyer and then a judge. Eventually, he became chief justice of the U.S. Supreme Court (1969–1986). As chief justice, Burger generally avoided controversy. He believed that the three branches of government must balance each other. He led the Court to an 8–0 decision requiring President Richard Nixon to turn over the tapes and memos related to the Watergate scandal, which Nixon wanted to keep private. The scandal ultimately led to Nixon's resignation.

**?** **Want to know more?** See www.michaelariens. com/ConLaw/justices/burger.htm

## THE JUDICIAL BRANCH

Judges and their courts make up the judicial branch of government. The judges' job is to apply the laws in making decisions on court cases. Most cases start in the district courts. Someone who thinks a mistake was made in a case can ask the court of appeals to review the decision. Minnesota's highest court is the state supreme court. It can review decisions made by the court of appeals. It's made up of a chief justice, or judge, and six associate justices. All of these judges are elected to six-year terms. Minnesota also has a special tax court and a workers' compensation court of appeals.

## LOCAL GOVERNMENT

Minnesota's counties, cities, and towns all have their own governments. Each of the state's 87 counties has a five- or seven-member board of commissioners. Other county officials usually include an attorney, an auditor, a treasurer, and a sheriff. Most cities elect a mayor and a city council.

Almost 1,800 communities are classified as towns, or townships. Once a year, their citizens come together in town meetings and elect a three- or five-member board of supervisors to handle town business. They also vote on local issues. For people in rural communities, town meetings are a great way to experience real democracy.

# Minnesota Counties

This map shows the 87 counties in Minnesota. St. Paul, the state capital,
is indicated with a star.

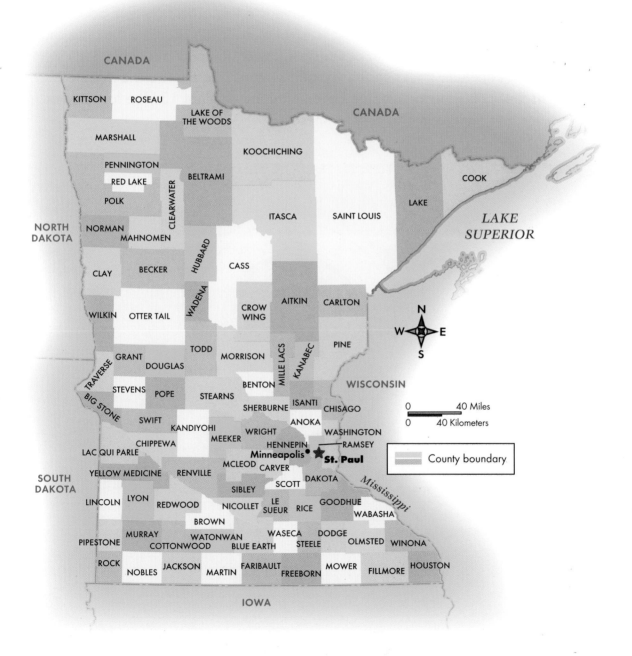

# State Flag

The Minnesota state flag was adopted in 1957. The three dates on the flag represent the year of Minnesota's first permanent white settlement (1819), the year of statehood (1858), and the year the original flag was adopted (1893). The Minnesota state flag is royal blue. In the center is the state seal. Around the seal is a wreath of the state flower, the pink and white lady's slipper. Nineteen stars ring the wreath, symbolizing the fact that Minnesota was the 19th state to enter the Union after the original 13. The largest star represents the North Star and Minnesota.

# State Seal

The first state seal of Minnesota, based on the seal used during territorial days, was adopted in 1858. It has been revised three times. The state seal combines symbols of Minnesota's agriculture (a man plowing a field in the foreground), lumber industry (a stump), and the state's Native American heritage (a Native American on horseback in the background). The state motto, *L'Etoile du Nord* (The Star of the North), runs across the top of the seal.

A worker inspects
freshly harvested
wheat in East
Grand Forks.

# CHAPTER EIGHT

# ECONOMY

★

**D**O YOU EAT CHEERIOS OR USE SCOTCH TAPE? If you do, you're playing a part in Minnesota's economy. These are just two of the thousands of goods the state produces. With its vast stretches of farmland, booming industrial plants, and rich mineral and forest resources, Minnesota has quite a diverse economy. Its goods and services are worth more than $240 billion a year. That's higher than the production figures for the country of Greece!

Shoppers at the amusement park inside
Bloomington's Mall of America

## SERVICE INDUSTRIES

Service industries make up the largest part of
Minnesota's economy. Service workers include people
who teach, repair bikes, drive trucks, serve food, and
help the sick. Health care workers make up a large
segment of Minnesota's service industry. Hundreds of
people work at Rochester's Mayo Clinic, which ranks
as one of the top hospitals in the United States. People
who work at retail stores are service workers, too.
Edina's Southdale Center was the nation's first indoor
shopping mall. Today, Bloomington's Mall of America
is one of the nation's largest.

# Major Agricultural and Mining Products

This map shows where Minnesota's major agricultural and mining products come from. See a chicken? That means poultry is found there.

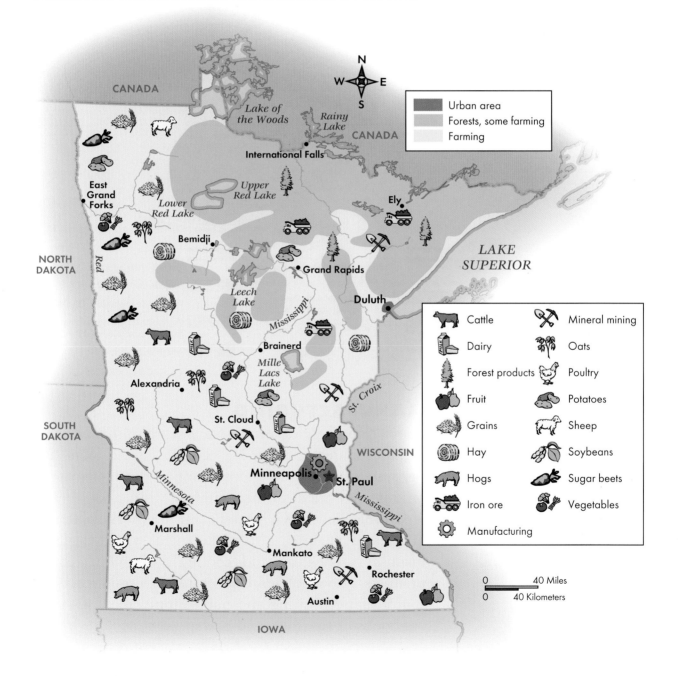

**Legend:**

Urban area
Forests, some farming
Farming

| | | | |
|---|---|---|---|
| Cattle | | Mineral mining | |
| Dairy | | Oats | |
| Forest products | | Poultry | |
| Fruit | | Potatoes | |
| Grains | | Sheep | |
| Hay | | Soybeans | |
| Hogs | | Sugar beets | |
| Iron ore | | Vegetables | |
| Manufacturing | | | |

0   40 Miles
0   40 Kilometers

# What Do Minnesotans Do?

This color-coded chart shows what industries Minnesotans work in.

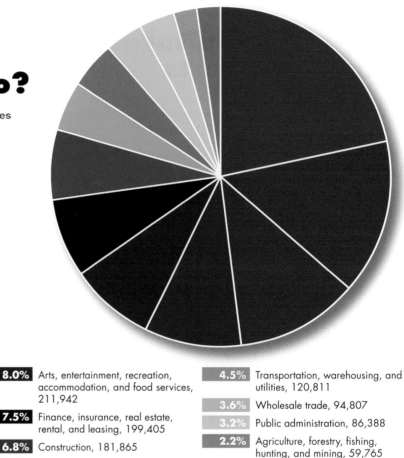

**21.8%** Educational services, health care, and social assistance, 579,814

**14.6%** Manufacturing, 389,190

**11.8%** Retail trade, 313,455

**9.1%** Professional, scientific, management, administrative and waste management services, 242,679

**8.0%** Arts, entertainment, recreation, accommodation, and food services, 211,942

**7.5%** Finance, insurance, real estate, rental, and leasing, 199,405

**6.8%** Construction, 181,865

**4.7%** Other services, except public administration, 123,988

**4.5%** Transportation, warehousing, and utilities, 120,811

**3.6%** Wholesale trade, 94,807

**3.2%** Public administration, 86,388

**2.2%** Agriculture, forestry, fishing, hunting, and mining, 59,765

**2.2%** Information, 58,739

Source: U.S. Census Bureau, 2005 estimate

**Canned in Minnesota, SPAM has its own fan club and Web site. An entire museum in Austin is dedicated to the canned meat.**

## MANUFACTURING

About 15 percent of Minnesotans work in manufacturing. Computer parts and electronics equipment are the state's top factory goods. Some of those electronic products are medical instruments. Minneapolis-based Medtronic developed pacemakers for heart patients. Minnesota factories also make metal products, farm machinery, heating and cooling equipment, paper products, snowmobiles, and petroleum products. The state's many printing and publishing companies turn out books, magazines, and newspapers.

Food processing is big business in the state. Minnesota is a national leader in meatpacking and cheese and milk production. Minnesotans also process milk into butter and ice cream. Much of Minnesota's wheat is processed into flour, and some of that flour ends up in cake mixes. Cereal and canned fruits and vegetables are some of the state's other processed foods.

SPAM could be Minnesota's most famous processed food. According to Austin manufacturer Hormel Foods, almost 7 billion cans of this meat product have been sold since it was invented in 1937. The company proudly boasts that three cans of SPAM are sold in the United States every second!

Many large manufacturing companies are headquartered in the Twin Cities area. General Mills, for example, is in the Minneapolis suburb of Golden Valley. The company's products include Pillsbury flour, Betty Crocker cake mixes, Old El Paso Mexican foods, Green Giant veg-

**Wheaties cereal was invented in 1921, when a worker accidentally spilled a wheat bran mixture onto a hot stove.**

**Q: WAS BETTY CROCKER A REAL PERSON?**

**A:** Betty was never a real person. Washburn-Crosby (now General Mills) invented her in 1921 as a symbol of quality and service.

A worker at a Minnesota egg-processing plant

### RICHARD W. SEARS: BUSINESS GENIUS

Richard W. Sears (1863–1914), a native of Stewartville, was a businessman who began selling watches in 1886. In 1893, he founded Sears, Roebuck and Company with his partner, Alvah C. Roebuck. The company produced a catalog that became required reading in rural homes around the nation. You could buy everything from clothing to bicycles to guns from the catalog. Sears eventually turned his mail-order business into one of the largest department store chains in the world.

**? Want to know more?** See www.bgsu.edu/departments/acs/1890s/sears/sears2.html

etables, and Cheerios and Wheaties cereals. The Target chain of stores is headquartered in Minneapolis. Maplewood, near St. Paul, is the home of 3M. This company makes Scotch Tape, Post-it Notes, and hundreds of other products. The electronics company Best Buy is centered in Richfield, a suburb of Minneapolis.

## AGRICULTURE

Minnesota is one of the country's top farming states. In fact, farms and pastures cover almost half of Minnesota's land area. Less than 3 percent of Minnesota's workers work on farms, though. Corn is the state's leading crop, followed by soybeans. Both of these crops are grown in southern Minnesota and are mainly used to feed livestock. Hay, barley, wheat, potatoes, peas, sugar beets, sunflower seeds, and oats are some other important Minnesota crops.

Farm-raised animals bring in millions of dollars' worth of farm income, too. Minnesota is one of the top states in hog and milk production. Minnesota farmers also produce beef cattle, turkeys, chickens, and eggs. In 2002, Minnesota raised more turkeys than any other state.

## MINING

Minnesota has been the nation's top producer of iron ore for more than 100 years. Today, however, most of the state's high-quality iron ore has been mined out. Most iron mining activities are now centered on extract-

Loading a truck with iron ore in Hibbing

ing taconite, a low-grade ore that contains only small amounts of iron. The taconite is ground up and processed to remove the iron. Even so, Minnesota still produces about three-fourths of the nation's iron ore.

Sand and gravel are mined in Minnesota, too. So are granite and limestone. All these minerals are used in the construction industry. Peat, the decayed remains of plants that built up over thousands of years, is con-

## SEE IT HERE!

### IRONWORLD DISCOVERY CENTER

Stop by the Ironworld Discovery Center in Chisholm. There you can tour a real taconite mine and see how taconite ore is mined and processed. First, you'll put on a hard hat. Then you'll head out to the mine, where you'll see massive bulldozers, gigantic shovels, and three-story trucks at work. At the Discovery Center's museum, you'll learn all about the history of Minnesota's iron industry. You'll also explore the lives of the immigrants and other miners who worked on the iron ranges.

## Top Products

| | |
|---|---|
| **Agriculture** | Corn, soybeans, hogs and pigs, dairy products, cattle and calves |
| **Manufacturing** | Computer and electronic equipment, food products, metal products, machinery |
| **Mining** | Iron ore, sand and gravel, crushed stone, granite, limestone, peat |
| **Forestry** | Lumber, wood pulp |
| **Fishing** | Walleye, yellow perch, lake trout |

These cut logs will be transported to a mill for processing into paper and lumber.

## WORD TO KNOW

**wood pulp** *wood that has been crushed and processed into a soft, moist material used for making paper and other products*

sidered a mining product. It's used as both a fertilizer and a fuel. Minnesota is a leading state in peat production. Most peat mining takes place in the northern half of the state.

## FORESTRY AND FISHING

Minnesota has many sawmills from its days as the nation's leading supplier of lumber. Forest trees are also processed into paper, **wood pulp**, and other wood products.

Thousands of people enjoy fishing in Minnesota's rivers and lakes. But fishing is an important commercial industry, too. Lake Superior yields lake herring and lake trout. Walleye, yellow perch, crappie, and carp are some of the catches on the inland lakes and rivers. Turtles and clams are valuable catches, too. Minnesota is a major supplier of turtle meat, and its clamshells are shipped to Asia to make cultured pearls.

## SHIPPING

Duluth, on Lake Superior, has one of the busiest inland ports in the country. Cargo ships pull in and out, carrying iron ore, farm products, and other goods. They go on to other Great Lakes ports or continue on the St. Lawrence Seaway to the Atlantic Ocean. Ore from Minnesota's iron mines is regularly shipped to steel mills in other states. The Mississippi, St. Croix, and Minnesota rivers are also important commercial waterways. Barges on these rivers transport tons of Minnesota grains and minerals.

**A tugboat escorts a cargo ship in the Duluth harbor.**

**SEE IT HERE!**

**STORA ENSO PAPER MILL**

How is paper made? You'll find out at the Stora Enso paper mill in Duluth. On a walk through the mill, you'll see continuous rolls of paper processed on massive machines towering high over your head. This mill specializes in making supercalendered paper. That's a smooth, glossy, thin type of paper used for magazines and catalogs.

TRAVEL GUIDE

# TRAVEL GUIDE

★

FROM THE NORTHERN WILDERNESS TO THE BUSTLING TWIN CITIES TO THE SOUTHERN PRAIRIE LANDS, MINNESOTA IS A GREAT PLACE TO EXPLORE. Hang out with lumberjacks at the Forest History Center, crawl inside a sod house, go deep underground into Niagara Cave, or hike to the top of Inspiration Peak. Whatever you enjoy, you're sure to find it in Minnesota. So let's hit the road!

← Follow along with this travel map. We'll begin in Alexandria, make our way around the state, and end up in Pipestone!

# NORTH CENTRAL/ WEST

**THINGS TO DO:** Step across the Mississippi River, sit on Paul Bunyan's lap, paddle your canoe across sparkling waters, spot a moose alongside a lake, and see a Viking ship!

## Alexandria

★ **Runestone Museum:** Did Vikings explore this area in the 1300s? In 1898, a farmer found a stone with old Scandinavian writing on it. Some people think it was a hoax. At this museum, you can see the stone, called the Kensington Runestone, and decide for yourself! And be sure to have your picture taken with Big Ole, the Viking statue that towers 28 feet (8.5 m) high.

Viking statue at the Runestone Museum

Statues of Paul Bunyan and Babe the Blue Ox in Bemidji

## Bemidji

★ **Paul Bunyan and Babe:** Check out these statues of the legendary lumberjack and his giant blue ox.

## Red Lake

★ **Upper and Lower Red Lakes:** See cranes, moose, and bears, or catch a walleye; you can also canoe or Jet Ski around these giant lakes.

## Brainerd

★ **More Paul Bunyans:** Gaze up at a statue of the giant lumberman at Paul Bunyan Land amusement park, see Paul and Babe by Brainerd's historic water tower, or sit on Bunyan's lap in front of the city's welcome center!

### Elk River

★ **Oliver Kelley Farm:** This working farm has costumed guides who demonstrate farming methods and portray family life of the 1850s.

### St. Cloud

★ **Munsinger Gardens:** Explore science and nature centers, gardens, orchards, and farms, and then enjoy a picnic along the Mississippi River!

### Baudette

★ **Willie Walleye:** This gigantic fish greets you as you head up to Lake of the Woods. This area is a great spot for camping, hiking, fishing, and bird-watching.

### Cass Lake

★ **Chippewa National Forest:** Hike or bike through this forest, which has the highest concentration of bald eagles in the country. Deer, foxes, and bears are just some of the other wildlife you might meet there.

### Bena

★ **Lake Winnibigoshish:** Locals just call it "Big Winnie." Here in the heart of Chippewa National Forest, you can lounge on a sandy beach or explore the lake along with the ducks and loons.

Visitors at Itasca State Park walking across the Mississippi River

### Lake Itasca

★ **Itasca State Park:** Lake Itasca is the source of the Mississippi River. Wade across the mighty river where it's just a little stream! Or you can tiptoe across on the stepping-stones. According to legend, anyone who steps across the Mississippi River at its source will live a long and fruitful life.

## FAQ

**Q8 HOW DID LAKE ITASCA GET ITS NAME?**

**A8** Explorer Henry Rowe Schoolcraft created the name from the Latin words *veritas* ("truth") and *caput* ("head"). He linked the syllables from *verITAS CAput* to create the word *Itasca*, signifying the "true head" of the Mississippi River.

## Urbank

★ **Inspiration Peak:** You'll find it along the Otter Trail Scenic Byway. Hike to the top and gaze around. According to author Sinclair Lewis, "There's to be seen a glorious 20-mile circle of some 50 lakes scattered among fields and pastures, like sequins fallen on an old paisley shawl."

Sinclair Lewis Boyhood Home

## MINI-BIO

## ROBERT ASP: HE DARED TO DREAM

Robert Asp (?–1980) was a guidance counselor at Moorhead Junior High. He dreamed of building a Viking ship and sailing it to Norway, his ancestors' homeland. He began building the ship (above) in an old potato warehouse in 1974. He finished it and sailed it on Lake Superior in 1980. Asp died later that year. In 1982, his children decided to make his dream come true. They sailed it all the way to Norway!

**? Want to know more?** See www.hjemkomst-center.com/ship/main.htm

## Sauk Centre

★ **Sinclair Lewis Boyhood Home:** Tour the home of America's first winner of the Nobel Prize for Literature. Then stroll the quiet streets of this town that was the model for Gopher Prairie in Lewis's novel *Main Street*.

## Moorhead

★ **Heritage Hjemkomst Interpretive Center:** Here you can see a life-size Viking ship (left) built by a school guidance counselor. Robert Asp modeled his ship after the *Gokstad*, a real Viking ship dating from 800 CE.

# NORTHEAST REGION

**THINGS TO DO:** Paddle through the northern waters, get a taste of lumberjack life, tour a paper mill, learn about commercial shipping, and howl with the wolves!

## International Falls

★ **Voyageurs National Park:** French Canadian explorers once canoed these scenic waters with loads of furs. Now you can canoe the same waterways and explore their many islands.

## Ely

★ **Boundary Waters Canoe Area Wilderness:** Ely is the place to get outfitted for your expedition into this watery wilderness. Pick up canoeing gear, food, and maps, and paddle out along hundreds of miles of lakes and streams.

★ **International Wolf Center:** At this site, you can watch wolves eat, sleep, play, and scuffle with one another. See the "Wolves and Humans" exhibit, learn how a wolf pack lives, and even learn to howl! Scientists here study wolf behavior to learn more about how wolf populations can survive in the wild.

★ **Cabin of the Root Beer Lady:** Dorothy Molter used to make 12,000 bottles of root beer a year to refresh canoeists. You can still visit her cabin, learn all about Dorothy, and guzzle down the frosty drink.

## Grand Marais

★ **Grand Portage National Monument:** This site on Lake Superior marks the location of a historic canoe route and a 1700s trading post for the British North West Company. Be sure to hike to the High Falls of the Pigeon River, the state's biggest waterfall. Spanning the border with Canada, it plunges almost 120 feet (37 m).

Visitors at the International Wolf Center

## The North Shore

★ **North Shore Drive:** This route along Lake Superior is known for its beautiful scenery. Look one way and see the craggy shoreline. Look the other way, and there are forested mountains. No wonder it's a favorite vacation area!

## Duluth

★ **Glensheen Estate:** Tour the ornate, 39-room mansion built by mining king Chester A. Congdon in 1905. Also see the gardens, carriage collection, boathouse, and more.

★ **Lake Superior Marine Museum:** Here you can learn all about commercial shipping on the upper Great Lakes through dozens of scale-model ships and interactive displays.

An Ojibwe exhibit at the North West Company Fur Post

## Pine City

★ **North West Company Fur Post:** At this site, a fur trade clerk explains how trading worked, and an Ojibwe woman takes you through her wigwam. Other costumed guides demonstrate daily life of the voyageurs.

## Grand Rapids

★ **Forest History Center:** Here you can see what life was like in a logging camp in 1900. Meet costumed guides portraying lumberjacks, blacksmiths, and other camp workers. Then hop aboard the wanigan (a floating cook shack) and climb a ranger's lookout tower.

## SEE IT HERE!

### EXPLORING UNDERWATER LIFE

Would you like to stroke a stingray or pet a sturgeon? Then check out the touch tank at Duluth's Great Lakes Aquarium! You can see otters playing and watch divers feeding the fish. In another area, you can sail a miniature ship through a model of the Great Lakes.

★ **Children's Discovery Museum:** At this museum, you can tour a kid-size river town, explore a dinosaur dig, locate your own home at Geo-Zoooom, and meet Tree-sa, the talking tree.

★ **Blandin Paper Mill:** Tour this mill to learn about forestry, logging, and the papermaking process.

Powwow at the Mille Lacs Indian Museum

## Onamia

★ **Mille Lacs Indian Museum:** Here you'll learn about the culture and history of the Mille Lacs band of Ojibwes. In the crafts room, you'll see demonstrations of traditional cooking, birch-bark basketry, and beadwork.

# TWIN CITIES METRO AREA

**THINGS TO DO:** Shop at the nation's biggest shopping mall, see hundreds of wild animals in their natural habitats, experience Minnesota pioneer life, and check out the world's largest ball of twine!

## Minneapolis

★ **Minnehaha Park:** Here you can picnic next to Minnehaha Falls—a 53-foot (16 m) waterfall right in the city. This waterfall inspired the poet Henry Wadsworth Longfellow to name Hiawatha's wife Minnehaha in *The Song of Hiawatha*.

★ **Minneapolis Sculpture Garden:** Don't miss its most photographed sculpture. *Spoonbridge and Cherry*, by Claes Oldenburg and Coosje van Bruggen, is a 5,800-pound (2,631 kilogram) spoon holding a 1,200-pound (544 kg) cherry!

*Spoonbridge and Cherry* sculpture in Minneapolis

★ **Minneapolis Institute of Arts:**
The largest art museum in
Minnesota, it features American,
European, Asian, and African art.

★ **Hubert H. Humphrey Metrodome:** Tour the stadium where the
Twins and the Vikings play. But
that's not all. The Metrodome hosts
college athletics, rock concerts, and
even in-line skating.

## FAQ

### Q8 WHAT WAS THE CITY OF ST. PAUL'S ORIGINAL NAME?

**A8** St. Paul was once called Pig's Eye! In 1838,
the fur trapper Pierre "Pig's Eye" Parrant built
a shack near today's downtown St. Paul and
operated a tavern there. The community that grew
up around the tavern was called Pig's Eye, after
Parrant. In 1841, a Catholic priest renamed the
settlement St. Paul.

### St. Paul

★ **Science Museum of Minnesota:**
Explore hundreds of science, technology, and natural history exhibits
at this museum. See bizarre medical instruments in its Museum of
Questionable Medical Devices. Or
watch a film in the Omnitheater,
where a domed screen surrounds
the audience.

★ **Minnesota History Center:** Here
you can learn about Minnesota's
history from the time of its earliest
settlers and communities through
the 20th century.

★ **Minnesota Children's Museum:**
Climb, splash, crawl, build, experi-
ment, and explore—you'll have
unforgettable adventures at this
world-class museum.

★ **Gibbs Museum of Pioneer and
Dakotah Life:** This 1800s farm site
offers a glimpse into early farm life
in Minnesota. Explore the farm-
house, schoolhouse, and barns, as
well as a tepee and a bark lodge.

### Fort Snelling

★ **Historic Fort Snelling:** Take a trip
back in time to see what life was
like almost 200 years ago. At this
restored 1820s military post, costumed guides demonstrate crafts
and military activities and put on
skits about everyday life at the fort.

A student taking notes at the Science Museum of
Minnesota

## SEE IT HERE!

### SHOP TILL YOU DROP

Bloomington's Mall of America is one of the nation's biggest shopping and entertainment centers. More people visit the mall every year than Florida's Walt Disney World and Arizona's Grand Canyon combined. People even fly in from countries around the world just to shop there. The mall's Camp Snoopy is a 7-acre (3 ha) theme park with 30 attractions, including a roller coaster, a Ferris wheel, and the Timberland Twister. There are bowling lanes, a Lego playroom, and dozens of restaurants, as well as more than 500 shops.

### Apple Valley

★ **Minnesota Zoo:** Roam the trails and meet tigers, kangaroos, and more than 2,300 other animals in their natural surroundings.

### Darwin

★ **Twine Ball Museum:** Here you can see the world's largest ball of twine. Francis Johnson made it. He spent four hours a day for 39 years winding the twine round and round. At one point, he needed a crane to hold it up while he kept winding. Now the ball is 12 feet (3.7 m) across and weighs 17,400 pounds (7,900 kg)!

# SOUTHERN REGION

**THINGS TO DO:** Explore a sod house, tour an underground cave, marvel at ancient rock carvings, and see where Indians got the stone for their peace pipes!

## Harmony

★ **Niagara Cave:** Explore one of the largest underground caverns in the country, complete with a 60-foot (18 m) waterfall.

## SEE IT HERE!

### HARMONY'S AMISH HERITAGE

Amish people began moving into Harmony in 1974. Now their community has grown to about 100 families, with three church districts and seven one-room schools. The Old Order Amish are devout Christians with strong beliefs that bind them together. In line with their faith, they dress plainly and live simple lives without modern conveniences such as cars and electricity. Instead, they travel in horse-drawn buggies, light their homes with kerosene lamps, and heat water on wood-burning stoves. The entire community joins together for harvests and barn- and house-building. Amish quilts, furniture, and baked goods are prized for their high quality.

Jesse James reenactment in Northfield

## Northfield

★ **Northfield Historical Society Museum:** This building was once the First National Bank. In 1876, townspeople foiled the Jesse James gang when they tried to rob the bank. Learn all about the rip-roaring raid in the museum's exhibits.

## Rochester

★ **Transparent Man:** See this life-size, see-through glass man to learn about what's inside your body. He stands in the Patient Education Center of Rochester's Mayo Clinic.

## New Ulm

★ **Glockenspiel:** Head to Schonlau Park Plaza at noon, 3:00 P.M., or 5:00 P.M. to enjoy this musical tower clock. That's when figures beneath the clock come out and perform!

## Mankato

★ **Betsy-Tacy Society:** Tour the childhood home of children's book author Maud Hart Lovelace and relive her daydreams as you stroll the neighborhood.

**MINI-BIO**

## MAUD HART LOVELACE: THE REAL BETSY

Maud Hart Lovelace (1892–1980) grew up in Mankato, and her best friend lived across the street. When Lovelace grew up, she wrote children's novels based on her childhood days. Called the Betsy-Tacy books, they feature two friends in the town of Deep Valley—Mankato in disguise! Today, visitors can tour Lovelace's childhood home and her best friend's house.

**?** **Want to know more?** See http://people.mnhs.org/authors/biog_detail.cfm?PersonID=love277

Laura Ingalls Wilder Museum

## Walnut Grove

★ **Laura Ingalls Wilder Museum:**
Located in the author's childhood
hometown, this museum highlights
her pioneer life and surroundings.
Exhibits include a little red schoolhouse, a doll collection, and items
from the *Little House on the Prairie*
TV series.

## Morton

★ **Lower Sioux Agency State
Historic Site:** This is where the
U.S.-Dakota War of 1862 began.
Learn the story behind the con-
flict, see a Dakota bark lodge, and
explore traditional Dakota life.

## Sanborn

★ **Sod House on the Prairie:**
Explore a "soddy" just like those
the pioneers lived in. For a realistic
experience, you can dress up in
pioneer clothes!

## Jeffers

★ **Jeffers Petroglyphs:** Native
peoples left more than 2,000 rock
carvings of people, deer, elk, buffalo, turtles, thunderbirds, and
other figures here. They tell a story
that spans almost 5,000 years,
beginning around 3000 BCE.

## Pipestone

★ **Pipestone National Monument:**
Here you'll see pipes carved by
Native Americans using the red
stone found in Pipestone's quarries.

A waterfall at Pipestone National Monument

# SCIENCE, TECHNOLOGY, & MATH PROJECTS

Make weather maps, graph population statistics, and research endangered species that live in the state.

## 120

# PRIMARY VS. SECONDARY SOURCES

## 121

So what are primary and secondary sources? And what's the diff? This section explains all that and where you can find them.

# BIOGRAPHICAL DICTIONARY

## 133

This at-a-glance guide highlights some of the state's most important and influential people. Visit this section and read about their contributions to the state, the country, and the world.

# RESOURCES

Books, Web sites, DVDs, and more. Take a look at these additional sources for information about the state.

## 137

# WRITING PROJECTS

★ ★ ★

## Create an Election Brochure or Web Site!

Run for office! Throughout this book you've read about some of the issues that concern Minnesota today.

★ Explain how you meet the qualifications to be governor of Minnesota, and talk about the three or four major issues you'll focus on if you're elected.

★ Remember, you'll be responsible for Minnesota's budget. How would you spend the taxpayers' money?

**SEE:** Chapter Seven, pages 84–90.

**GO TO:** Minnesota's government Web site at www.state.mn.us to learn more about the state government. You might also want to read some local newspapers. Try these:
*Minneapolis Star Tribune* at www.startribune.com
*Duluth News Tribune* at www.duluthnewstribune.com
*Rochester Post-Bulletin* at www.postbulletin.com

## Compare and Contrast —When, Why, and How Did They Come?

Compare the migration and explorations of the first Native people and the first European explorers. Tell about:

★ when their migrations began
★ how they traveled
★ why they migrated
★ where their journeys began and ended
★ what they found when they arrived

**SEE:** Chapters Two and Three, pages 22–41.

## Write a Memoir, Journal, or Editorial for Your School Newspaper!

**Picture Yourself . . .**

★ Research various famous Minnesotans, such as Jesse Ventura, Jessica Biel, Laura Ingalls Wilder, Roger Maris, Kirby Puckett, and many others.

★ Based on your research, pick one person you would most like to talk with.

★ Write a script of the interview. What questions would you ask? How would this person answer? Create a question-and-answer format. You may want to supplement this writing project with a voice-recording dramatization of the interview.

**SEE:** Chapter Six, pages 76–83, or the Biographical Dictionary on pages 133–136.

**GO TO:** The Minnesota Historical Society Web site at www.mnhs.org to find out more about public figures from Minnesota.

Kirby Puckett

# ART PROJECTS

★  ★  ★

## Create a PowerPoint Presentation or Visitors' Guide

**Welcome to Minnesota!**

Minnesota's a great place to visit and to live! From its natural beauty to its historical sites, there's plenty to see and do. In your PowerPoint presentation or brochure, highlight 10 to 15 of Minnesota's fascinating landmarks. Be sure to include:

★ a map of the state showing where these sites are located

★ photos, illustrations, Web links, natural history facts, geographic stats, climate and weather, plants and wildlife, and recent discoveries

**SEE:** Chapters One and Nine, pages 8–21 and 104–115.

**GO TO:** A Web site about Minnesota tourism at www.exploreminnesota.com. Download and print maps, photos, national landmark images, and vacation ideas for tourists.

## Illustrate the Lyrics to the Minnesota State Song

**("Hail! Minnesota")**

Use markers, paints, photos, collages, colored pencils, or computer graphics to illustrate the lyrics to "Hail! Minnesota," the state song. Turn your illustrations into a picture book, or scan them into PowerPoint presentation and add music!

**SEE:** The lyrics to "Hail! Minnesota" on page 128.

**GO TO:** The Minnesota state Web site at www. state.mn.us to find out more about the origin of Minnesota's state song.

## Research Minnesota's State Quarter

From 1999 to 2008, the U.S. Mint introduced new quarters commemorating each of the 50 states in the order they were admitted into the Union. Each state's quarter features a unique design on its reverse, or back.

**GO TO:** www.usmint.gov/kids and find out what's featured on the back of the Minnesota quarter.

Research and write an essay explaining:

★ the significance of each image

★ who designed the quarter

★ who chose the final design

Design your own Minnesota state quarter. What images would you choose for the reverse?

Make a poster showing the Minnesota quarter and label each image.

# SCIENCE, TECHNOLOGY, & MATH PROJECTS

★ ★ ★

## Graph Population Statistics!

★ Compare population statistics (such as ethnic background, birth, death, and literacy rates) in Minnesota counties or major cities.

★ On your graph or chart, look at population density, and write sentences describing what the population statistics show; graph one set of population statistics, and write a paragraph explaining what the graphs reveal.

**SEE:** Chapter Six, pages 66–74.

**GO TO:** The official Web site for the U.S. Census Bureau at www.census.gov, and at quickfacts. census.gov/qfd/states/27000.html, to find out more about population statistics, how they work, and what the statistics are for Minnesota.

## Track Endangered Species

Using your knowledge of Minnesota's wildlife, research what animals and plants are endangered or threatened. Find out what the state is doing to protect these species. Chart known populations of the animals and plants, and report on changes in certain geographic areas.

**SEE:** Chapter One, pages 18–21.

**GO TO:** The U.S. Fish and Wildlife site at www.fws. gov/midwest/endangered/lists/minnesot-spp.html or other Minnesota-specific sites.

## Create a Weather Map of Minnesota!

Use your knowledge of Minnesota's geography to research and identify conditions that result in specific weather events such as record cold temperatures. Create a weather map or poster that shows the weather patterns across the state. Include a caption explaining the technology used to measure weather phenomena.

**SEE:** Chapter One, pages 8–18.

**GO TO:** The National Oceanic and Atmospheric Administration's National Weather Service Web site at www.weather.gov for weather maps and forecasts for Minnesota.

A blizzard in Brainerd

# PRIMARY VS. SECONDARY SOURCES

★   ★   ★

## What's the Diff?

**Your teacher may require at least one or two primary sources and one or two secondary sources for your assignment.** So, what's the difference between the two?

★ **Primary sources are original.** You are reading the actual words of someone's diary, journal, letter, autobiography, or interview. Primary sources can also be photographs, maps, prints, cartoons, news/film footage, posters, first-person newspaper articles, drawings, musical scores, and recordings. By the way, when you conduct a survey, interview someone, shoot a video, or take photographs to include in a project, you are creating primary sources!

★ **Secondary sources are what you find in encyclopedias, textbooks, articles, biographies, and almanacs.** These are written by a person or group of people who tell about something that happened to someone else. Secondary sources also recount what another person said or did. This book is an example of a secondary source.

## Now that you know what primary sources are—where can you find them?

★ **Your school or local library:** Check the library catalog for collections of original writings, government documents, musical scores, and so on. Some of this material may be stored on microfilm. The Library of Congress Web site (www.loc.gov) is an excellent online resource for primary source materials.

★ **Historical societies:** These organizations keep historical documents, photographs, and other materials. Staff members can help you find what you are looking for. History museums are also great places to see primary sources firsthand.

★ **The Internet:** There are lots of sites that have primary sources you can download and use in a project or assignment.

# TIMELINE

★   ★   ★

**U.S. Events** `1600` **Minnesota Events**

**1600s**
Ojibwes migrate into what is now Minnesota.

**1620**
Pilgrims found Plymouth Colony, the second permanent English settlement.

**c. 1659**
French fur traders Pierre-Esprit Radisson and Médard Chouart, Sieur des Groseilliers, become the first Europeans to reach Minnesota.

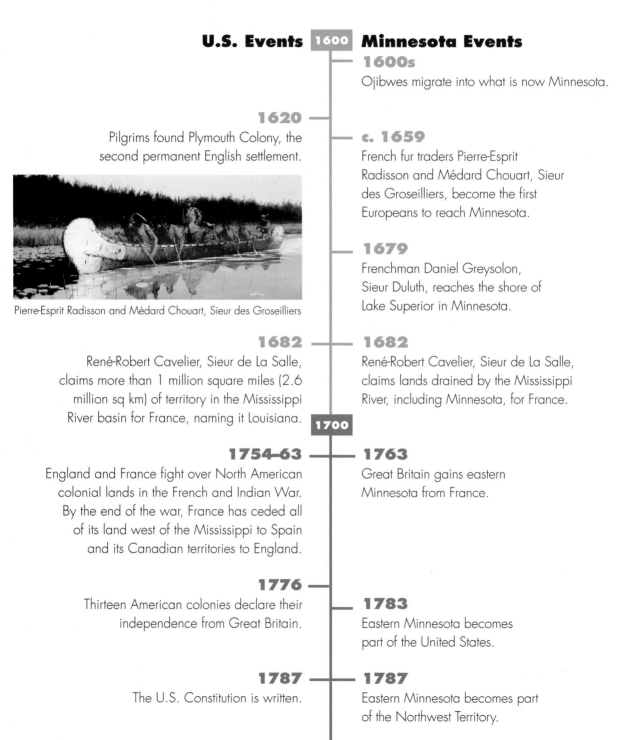

Pierre-Esprit Radisson and Médard Chouart, Sieur des Groseilliers

**1679**
Frenchman Daniel Greysolon, Sieur Duluth, reaches the shore of Lake Superior in Minnesota.

**1682**
René-Robert Cavelier, Sieur de La Salle, claims more than 1 million square miles (2.6 million sq km) of territory in the Mississippi River basin for France, naming it Louisiana.

**1682**
René-Robert Cavelier, Sieur de La Salle, claims lands drained by the Mississippi River, including Minnesota, for France.

`1700`

**1754–63**
England and France fight over North American colonial lands in the French and Indian War. By the end of the war, France has ceded all of its land west of the Mississippi to Spain and its Canadian territories to England.

**1763**
Great Britain gains eastern Minnesota from France.

**1776**
Thirteen American colonies declare their independence from Great Britain.

**1783**
Eastern Minnesota becomes part of the United States.

**1787**
The U.S. Constitution is written.

**1787**
Eastern Minnesota becomes part of the Northwest Territory.

## U.S. Events | **1800** | Minnesota Events

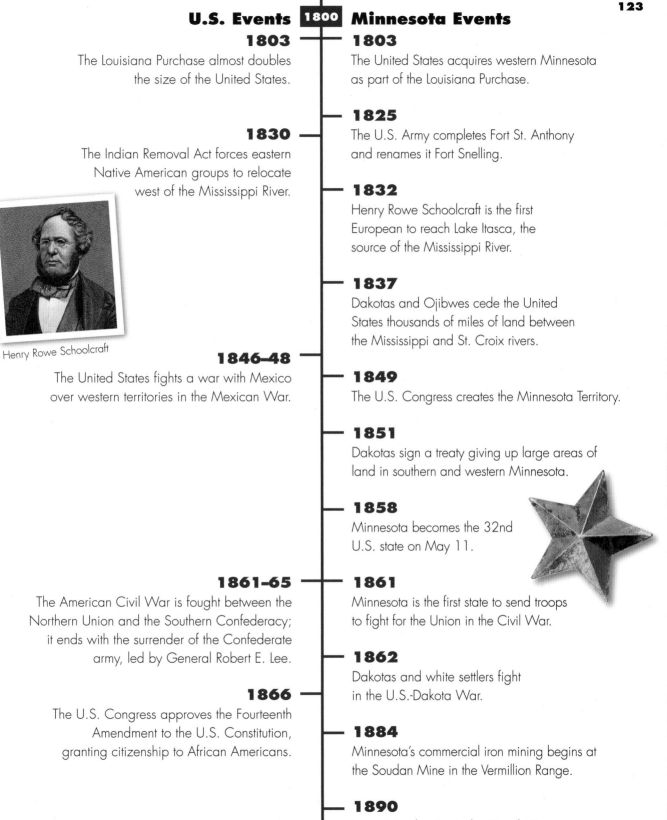

**U.S. Events**

### 1803
The Louisiana Purchase almost doubles the size of the United States.

### 1830
The Indian Removal Act forces eastern Native American groups to relocate west of the Mississippi River.

Henry Rowe Schoolcraft

### 1846–48
The United States fights a war with Mexico over western territories in the Mexican War.

### 1861–65
The American Civil War is fought between the Northern Union and the Southern Confederacy; it ends with the surrender of the Confederate army, led by General Robert E. Lee.

### 1866
The U.S. Congress approves the Fourteenth Amendment to the U.S. Constitution, granting citizenship to African Americans.

**Minnesota Events**

### 1803
The United States acquires western Minnesota as part of the Louisiana Purchase.

### 1825
The U.S. Army completes Fort St. Anthony and renames it Fort Snelling.

### 1832
Henry Rowe Schoolcraft is the first European to reach Lake Itasca, the source of the Mississippi River.

### 1837
Dakotas and Ojibwes cede the United States thousands of miles of land between the Mississippi and St. Croix rivers.

### 1849
The U.S. Congress creates the Minnesota Territory.

### 1851
Dakotas sign a treaty giving up large areas of land in southern and western Minnesota.

### 1858
Minnesota becomes the 32nd U.S. state on May 11.

### 1861
Minnesota is the first state to send troops to fight for the Union in the Civil War.

### 1862
Dakotas and white settlers fight in the U.S.-Dakota War.

### 1884
Minnesota's commercial iron mining begins at the Soudan Mine in the Vermillion Range.

### 1890
Iron mining begins in the Mesabi Range.

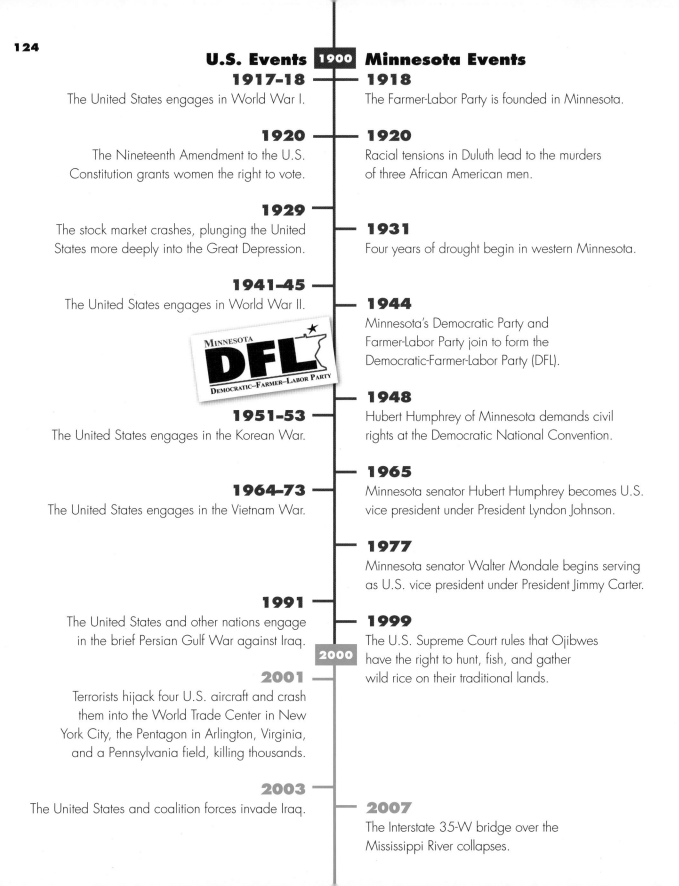

## U.S. Events  **1900**  Minnesota Events

**1917–18**
The United States engages in World War I.

**1918**
The Farmer-Labor Party is founded in Minnesota.

**1920**
The Nineteenth Amendment to the U.S. Constitution grants women the right to vote.

**1920**
Racial tensions in Duluth lead to the murders of three African American men.

**1929**
The stock market crashes, plunging the United States more deeply into the Great Depression.

**1931**
Four years of drought begin in western Minnesota.

**1941–45**
The United States engages in World War II.

**1944**
Minnesota's Democratic Party and Farmer-Labor Party join to form the Democratic-Farmer-Labor Party (DFL).

**1948**
Hubert Humphrey of Minnesota demands civil rights at the Democratic National Convention.

**1951–53**
The United States engages in the Korean War.

**1964–73**
The United States engages in the Vietnam War.

**1965**
Minnesota senator Hubert Humphrey becomes U.S. vice president under President Lyndon Johnson.

**1977**
Minnesota senator Walter Mondale begins serving as U.S. vice president under President Jimmy Carter.

**1991**
The United States and other nations engage in the brief Persian Gulf War against Iraq.

**1999**
The U.S. Supreme Court rules that Ojibwes have the right to hunt, fish, and gather wild rice on their traditional lands.

**2000**

**2001**
Terrorists hijack four U.S. aircraft and crash them into the World Trade Center in New York City, the Pentagon in Arlington, Virginia, and a Pennsylvania field, killing thousands.

**2003**
The United States and coalition forces invade Iraq.

**2007**
The Interstate 35-W bridge over the Mississippi River collapses.

# GLOSSARY

★  ★  ★

**abolitionists** people who were opposed to slavery and worked to end it

**archaeologists** people who study the remains of past human societies

**Archaic** relating to the early, formative phases of a culture

**breechcloths** garments worn by men over their lower bodies

**census** an official count of the population

**civil rights** basic rights that are guaranteed to all people under the U.S. Constitution

**discrimination** unequal treatment based on race, gender, religion, or other factors

**Emancipation Proclamation** an order freeing slaves in the Southern states, issued by President Abraham Lincoln on January 1, 1863

**glaciers** slow-moving masses of ice

**gristmill** a water-powered mill where grain is ground into flour

**lynching** to kill by mob without a lawful trial

**missionary** a person who tries to convert others to a religion

**portages** land trails used to carry canoes between rivers and lakes, or around waterfalls and rapids

**precipitation** all water that falls to the earth, including rain, sleet, hail, snow, dew, fog, and mist

**prophecy** a statement or story predicting a future event

**quarries** wide, open holes from which stone or minerals are dug

**reservations** lands set aside for Native Americans to live on

**Soviet Union** a former nation in eastern Europe and northern and central Asia; in 1991, it broke apart into 15 smaller countries, including Russia

**vaccinate** to administer medicine that protects against a particular disease

**wood pulp** wood that has been crushed and processed into a soft, moist material used for making paper and other products

# FAST FACTS

★ ★ ★

## State Symbols

| | |
|---|---|
| **Statehood date** | May 11, 1858, the 32nd state |
| **Origin of state name** | From Dakota words meaning "cloudy water" or "sky-tinted water," describing the Minnesota River |
| **State capital** | St. Paul |
| **State nickname** | Land of 10,000 Lakes |
| **State motto** | *L'Etoile du Nord* (The Star of the North) |
| **State bird** | Common loon |
| **State flower** | Pink and white lady's slipper |
| **State fish** | Walleye |
| **State gem** | Lake Superior agate |
| **State song** | "Hail! Minnesota" |
| **State tree** | Norway pine |
| **State fair** | Late August–early September near St. Paul |

State seal

## Geography

| | |
|---|---|
| **Total area; rank** | 86,939 square miles (225,171 sq km); 12th |
| **Land; rank** | 79,610 square miles (206,189 sq km); 14th |
| **Water; rank** | 7,329 square miles (18,982 sq km); 8th |
| **Inland water; rank** | 4,783 square miles (12,388 sq km); 3rd |
| **Great Lakes; rank** | 2,546 square miles (6,594 sq km); 5th |
| **Geographic center** | Crow Wing, 10 miles (16 km) southwest of Brainerd |
| **Longitude** | 89° 34' W to 97° 12' W |
| **Latitude** | 43° 34' N to 49° 23' N |
| **Highest point** | Eagle Mountain at 2,301 feet (701 m) |
| **Lowest point** | Lake Superior at 601 feet (183 m) |
| **Largest city** | Minneapolis |
| **Number of counties** | 87 |

# Population

| | |
|---|---|
| **Population; rank (2006 estimate)** | 5,167,101; 21st |
| **Density (2006 estimate)** | 65 persons per square mile (25 per sq km) |
| **Population distribution (2000 census)** | 71% urban, 29% rural |
| **Ethnic distribution (2005 estimate)** | White persons: 89.6%* |
| | Black persons: 4.3%* |
| | Asian persons: 3.4%* |
| | American Indian and Alaska Native persons: 1.2%* |
| | Native Hawaiian and Other Pacific Islanders: 0.1%* |
| | Persons reporting two or more races: 1.4% |
| | Persons of Hispanic or Latino origin: 3.6%† |
| | White persons not Hispanic: 86.3% |

*Includes persons reporting only one race.*
† *Hispanics may be of any race, so they are also included in applicable race categories.*

# Weather

| | |
|---|---|
| **Record high temperature** | 114°F (46°C) at Beardsley on July 29, 1917, and at Moorhead on July 6, 1936 |
| **Record low temperature** | −60°F (−51°C) at Tower on February 2, 1996 |
| **Average July temperature** | 73°F (23°C) |
| **Average January temperature** | 13°F (−11°C) |
| **Average yearly precipitation** | 29 inches (74 cm) |

State flag

# STATE SONG

★ ★ ★

## "Hail! Minnesota"

Words by Truman E. Rickard and Arthur E. Upson (1904)
Music by Truman E. Rickard

The song was originally the University of Minnesota's official hymn. The state legislature made it the official state song in 1945. The only modification is in the second line where "college dear" was changed to "our State so dear!"

Minnesota, hail to thee!
Hail to thee our state so dear!
Thy light shall ever be
A beacon bright and clear.
Thy sons and daughters true
Will proclaim thee near and far.
They will guard thy fame
And adore thy name;
Thou shalt be their Northern Star.

Like the stream that bends to sea,
Like the pine that seeks the blue,
Minnesota, still for thee,
Thy sons are strong and true.
From their woods and waters fair,
From their prairies waving far,
At thy call they throng,
With their shout and song,
Hailing thee their Northern Star.

# NATURAL AREAS AND HISTORIC SITES

★ ★ ★

### National Monuments

*Grand Portage National Monument* is the site of a major 18th-century fur-trading center. Visitors can see a canoe house, a rebuilt great hall, and Grand Portage.

*Pipestone National Monument* offers visitors a chance to see pipestone quarries and tallgrass prairies on 283 acres (115 ha) of scenic Minnesota land.

### National Park

*Voyageurs*, near International Falls, was formed by glaciers. Its varied landscape includes beaver ponds, islands, and swamps.

### National River and Recreation Area

*Mississippi National River and Recreation Area* provides visitors with views of the beginning of the largest river in the United States, as well as recreational areas along the river.

### National Scenic Trail

*North Country National Scenic Trail* traverses woods, prairies, and mountains, including several hundred miles through woods and waterways in Minnesota.

### National Scenic Riverway

*St. Croix National Scenic Riverway* is 252 miles (406 km) long and was one of the first riverways designated as Wild and Scenic by the National Park Service.

### State Parks

Minnesota has 67 state parks, all designed to preserve the state's landscape. *St. Croix State Park* has plenty to offer hikers, bikers, canoeists, horseback riders, campers, skiers, snowmobilers, and fishers. *Fort Snelling State Park* in the Twin Cities provides opportunities for biking and hiking along the Mississippi and Minnesota rivers, as well as a chance to see old Fort Snelling.

# SPORTS TEAMS

★ ★ ★

### NCAA Teams (Division I)
University of Minnesota *Golden Gophers*

# PROFESSIONAL SPORTS TEAMS

★ ★ ★

### Major League Baseball
Minnesota *Twins*

### National Hockey League
Minnesota *Wild*

### National Basketball Association
Minnesota *Timberwolves*

### Women's National Basketball Association
Minnesota *Lynx*

### National Football League
Minnesota *Vikings*

# CULTURAL INSTITUTIONS

★ ★ ★

## Libraries

The *Minnesota Historical Society Library and Collections* offers visitors a history of the state through a photograph collection that dates back to 1850.

The *Minnesota Indian Women's Resource Center* in Minneapolis provides information relating to American Indian women, including parenting advice and local Native American history.

At the *Minnesota Valley Regional Library* in Mankato, children will enjoy the children's reading room dedicated to author Maud Hart Lovelace, who is a native of Mankato.

## Museums

*Great Lakes Aquarium* (Duluth) is the only all-freshwater aquarium in the United States. Exhibits focus on the history and wildlife of Lake Superior.

The *Mill City Museum* (Minneapolis) chronicles the flour-milling industry that dominated world flour production for roughly a half century and fueled the growth of Minneapolis.

The *Mille Lacs Indian Museum* (Onamia) offers exhibits dedicated to telling the story of the Mille Lacs people.

The *Minneapolis Institute of Arts* houses 85,000 pieces of art and has collections ranging from ancient textiles to modern American art.

The *St. Louis County Heritage and Arts Center*, also known as the Duluth Depot, is a renovated train station that houses several art galleries and museums.

The *Science Museum of Minnesota* (St. Paul) opened in 1907. It has many exhibits related to science, along with a giant-screen Omnitheater.

The *Walker Art Center* (Minneapolis) has a world-renowned art museum, sculpture garden, and theater for performing arts.

## Performing Arts

Minnesota has two major symphony orchestras, two major dance companies, and two professional theater companies.

## Universities and Colleges

In 2006, Minnesota had 43 public and 55 private institutions of higher learning.

# ANNUAL EVENTS

## January–March

**Grand Vinterslass Fest** in Grand Rapids (January)

**Icebox Days winter festival** in International Falls (January)

**John Beargrease Sled Dog Race** between Duluth and Grand Marais (January)

**St. Paul Winter Carnival** (late January–early February)

**Duluth Winter Sports Festival** (January–February)

**International Eelpout Festival** in Walker (February)

**Voyageur Winter Festival** in Ely (February)

**Minnesota Finlandia Ski Marathon** in Bemidji (February)

## April–June

**Festival of Nations** in St. Paul (April or May)

**Swayed Pines Folk Fest** in Collegeville (April)

**Cinco de Mayo** in St. Paul (May)

**Grandma's Marathon** in Duluth (June)

**Wheels, Wings & Water Festival** in St. Cloud (June)

## July–September

**Art in the Park** in Albert Lea (July)

**Heritagefest** in New Ulm (July)

**Taste of Minnesota food festival** in St. Paul (July)

**Minneapolis Aquatennial** (July)

**Bayfront Blues Festival** in Duluth (August)

**Ethnic Days** in Chisholm (August)

**Fishermen's Picnic** in Grand Marais (August)

**Fringe Festival** in Minneapolis (August)

**Minnesota State Fair** near St. Paul (August–September)

**Dakota Public Powwow** in Mankato (September)

**Dozinky: A Czechoslovakian Harvest Festival** in New Prague (September)

**Western Minnesota Steam Threshers Reunion** in Rollag (September)

## October–December

**Oktoberfest** in New Ulm (October)

**Fish House Parade** in Aitkin (November)

**Folkways of Christmas** in Shakopee (December)

**Christmas in the Village** in Montevideo (December)

The **Andrews Sisters** were a popular singing group in the 1940s. **LaVerne (1911–1967)** and **Maxene (1916–1995)** were born in Minneapolis, and **Patty (1918–)** was born in Mound. They sold more recordings than any other female group in the history of pop music.

**Robert Asp** See page 108.

**Ann Bancroft (1955–)**, born in Mendota Heights, was the first woman to reach both the North Pole (1986) and the South Pole (1993).

**Charles Bender (1884–1954)**, a pitcher in the major leagues, invented the slider—a pitch halfway between a fastball and a curve. Part Ojibwe, he was born in Crow Wing County.

**Patricia Jane (Patty) Berg (1918–2006)**, born in Minneapolis, was a founder of the U.S. Ladies Professional Golf Association (LPGA) and won dozens of golf tournaments.

**Jessica Biel (1982–)** is an actor known for her roles on TV's *7th Heaven* and films such as *The Illusionist*. She was born in Ely.

**Harry Blackmun (1908–1999)** was an associate justice of the U.S. Supreme Court (1970–1994). He grew up in St. Paul.

**Norman Borlaug (1914–)**, a former professor at the University of Minnesota, developed hardy, superproductive varieties of wheat that helped increase world food production in the 1940s through the 1960s. In 1970, he was awarded the Nobel Peace Prize.

Charles Bender

**Herb Brooks (1937–2003)** led the University of Minnesota hockey team to three championships in the 1970s. He coached the U.S. Olympic hockey team when it won the gold medal in 1980 and the silver medal in 2002. Brooks was born in St. Paul.

**Warren Burger** See page 90.

**Mary Casanova (1957–)** is a children's book author whose award-winning books include *Moose Tracks*, *Riot*, and *One-Dog Canoe*. She was born in Duluth and lives near Ranier.

**Joel (1954–)** and **Ethan (1957–) Coen** are brothers and award-winning filmmakers whose movies include *O Brother, Where Art Thou?* and *Raising Arizona*. They are from St. Louis Park, a suburb of Minneapolis.

**Frances Densmore** See page 78.

**Kate DiCamillo (1964–)** is a children's book author whose popular novels include *Because of Winn-Dixie*, *The Tiger Rising*, and the Mercy Watson series. Born in Pennsylvania, she later moved to Minneapolis.

Jessica Biel

**William O. Douglas (1898–1980)** was a justice on the U.S. Supreme Court for 36 years (1939–1975). As of 2008, he was the longest-serving Supreme Court justice in U.S. history. He was born in Maine, Minnesota.

**Bob Dylan (1941–)** is a singer and songwriter. He was born in Duluth as Robert Allen Zimmerman and spent much of his childhood in Hibbing.

**Kimberly Elise (1967–)** is an actor whose movie credits include *Beloved*, *The Manchurian Candidate*, and *Diary of a Mad Black Woman*. She was born in Minneapolis.

**F. Scott Fitzgerald (1896–1940)** wrote novels and short stories about American life in the Jazz Age of the 1920s, including *The Great Gatsby*. He was born in St. Paul.

**James Earle Fraser (1876–1953)** was a sculptor who portrayed Native American subjects in works such as *End of the Trail*. He was born in Winona.

**Wanda Gág** See page 81.

**Judy Garland (1922–1969)** was a singer and actor who played Dorothy in the 1939 movie *The Wizard of Oz*. She was born in Grand Rapids as Frances Ethel Gumm.

Kimberly Elise

**J. Paul Getty (1892–1976)**, the founder of Getty Oil Company, was one of the first people in the world to amass $1 billion. He was born in Minneapolis.

**Cass Gilbert (1859–1934)** was an architect. He designed skyscrapers, museums, the U.S. Supreme Court building, and several state capitols, including Minnesota's. He grew up in St. Paul.

**Mary GrandPré (1954–)** illustrated the U.S. editions of the Harry Potter books. Born in South Dakota, she attended the Minneapolis College of Art and Design.

**Duane Hanson (1925–1996)** was a sculptor known for his life-size human figures. He was born in Alexandria.

**Josh Hartnett (1978–)** is an actor whose movie credits include *Black Hawk Down* and *Pearl Harbor*. He grew up in St. Paul.

**Hubert H. Humphrey** See page 88.

**Jerry Juhl (1958–2005)** was a puppeteer and writer. He wrote for TV series such as *Sesame Street*, *The Muppet Show*, and *Fraggle Rock*. He was born in St. Paul.

**Maude Kegg** See page 28.

**Garrison Keillor (1942–)** is a humorist and author. Since 1974, he has been the host of the live radio show *A Prairie Home Companion*. He was born in Anoka.

**T. R. Knight (1973–)** is an actor who plays the role of Dr. George O'Malley in the TV drama *Grey's Anatomy*. He was born in Minneapolis.

**Cornelia "Coya" Knutson (1912–1996)** was Minnesota's first woman to serve in the U.S. House of Representatives (1955–1959). Born in North Dakota, she attended Concordia College in Moorhead and later lived in Oklee.

**Winona LaDuke (1959–)**, an Ojibwe activist, campaigns for the return of lands to Native Americans. In 1996 and 2000, she was the vice presidential candidate on the Green Party's ticket.

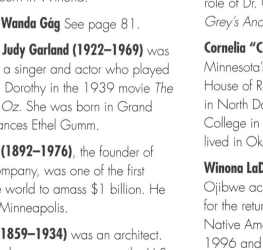

Winona LaDuke

**Jessica Lange (1949–)** is a an actor who won Academy Awards for her performances in *Tootsie* (1982) and *Blue Sky* (1994). She was born in Cloquet.

**Erik Larsen (1962–)** is a comic book illustrator and writer who contributed to the comics *The Amazing Spider-Man*, *Fantastic Four*, and others. He was born in Minneapolis.

**Greg LeMond (1961–)** is a professional bicycle racer. In 1986, he was the first American cyclist to win the Tour de France. He won again in 1989 and 1990. He lives in Medina.

Greg LeMond

**Sinclair Lewis (1885–1951)**, native of Sauk Centre, was the first American to win the Nobel Prize for Literature.

**Maud Hart Lovelace** See page 114.

**John Madden (1936–)** is a TV commentator for football games. He coached the Oakland Raiders from 1969 to 1978. Born in Austin, he was inducted into the Pro Football Hall of Fame in 2006.

**Roger Maris (1934–1985)** made Major League Baseball history in 1961, when he hit 61 home runs in a single season. Maris was born in Hibbing.

**E. G. Marshall (1914–1998)** was an actor who won two Emmy Awards for his role in the TV series *The Defenders*. He was born in Owatonna as Everett Eugene Grunz.

**Charles H. (1865–1939)** and **William J. (1861–1939) Mayo** were doctors. With their father, Dr. William Worrall Mayo, they founded the Mayo Clinic in Rochester in 1883.

**Eugene J. (Gene) McCarthy (1916–2005)**, born in Watkins, represented Minnesota in the U.S. House of Representatives (1949–1959) and the U.S. Senate (1959–1971).

**Frederick L. McGhee (1861–1912)**, Minnesota's first black lawyer, helped found the Niagara Movement of 1905, a forerunner of the National Association for the Advancement of Colored People (NAACP).

**Kate Millett (1934–)** is an author and activist for women's rights. Her 1970 book *Sexual Politics* was a groundbreaking work in feminist theory. She was born in St. Paul.

**Walter F. Mondale (1928–)**, a native of Ceylon, served as U.S. vice president under President Jimmy Carter (1977–1981). He also represented Minnesota in the U.S. Senate (1964–1976) and served as U.S. ambassador to Japan (1993–1996).

**Mee Moua (1969–)** was born in Laos and moved to the United States as a child. She was elected to the Minnesota senate in 2002.

**Sigurd Olson** See page 13.

**Alan Page (1945–)** is a former football player with the Minnesota Vikings (1967–1978) and the Chicago Bears (1978–1981). In 1993, he became an associate justice on Minnesota's supreme court.

Alan Page

**Gary Paulsen (1939–)** writes books for both young people and adults. He was born in Minneapolis.

**Jeannette Piccard (1895–1981)** was the world's first licensed female balloon pilot. In 1974, she became one of the first female Episcopal priests. She lived in Minneapolis.

Prince

**Charles Pillsbury** See page 54.

**Prince (1958–)** is a musician whose style combines rhythm and blues, rock, funk, jazz, and hip-hop. He was born in Minneapolis as Prince Rogers Nelson.

**Kirby Puckett (1960–2006)** was the longtime center fielder for the Minnesota Twins. He was elected to the National Baseball Hall of Fame in 2001.

**Marsha Qualey (1953–)** writes books for children and young adults. Her young-adult novels include *Just Like That*, *Too Big a Storm*, and *Thin Ice*. She was born in Austin.

**Jane Russell (1921–)** is a movie actor who was popular in the 1940s and 1950s. Her movies include *Gentlemen Prefer Blondes*. She was born in Bemidji.

**Winona Ryder (1971–)** is an actor who won a Golden Globe Award in 1994 for her performance in *The Age of Innocence*. Born Winona Laura Horowitz near Winona, she was named after that city.

**Henry Rowe Schoolcraft** See page 46.

**Charles Schulz** See page 82.

**Dred Scott** See page 49.

**Richard W. Sears** See page 100.

**Kevin Sorbo (1958–)** is an actor who played Hercules in the TV series *Hercules: The Legendary Journeys*. He was born in Mound.

**Heidemarie Stefanyshyn-Piper (1963–)** is an astronaut, engineer, and U.S. Navy officer. She was born in St. Paul.

**Taoyateduta** See page 52.

**Fran Tarkenton (1940–)** is a former quarterback with the Minnesota Vikings football team (1961–1966; 1972–1978). He was inducted into the Pro Football Hall of Fame in 1986.

**Jesse Ventura (1951–)**, a former professional wrestler, served as Minnesota's governor from 1999 to 2003. He was born in Minneapolis as James George Janos.

**DeWitt Wallace (1889–1981)** founded *Reader's Digest* magazine in 1922. He was born in St. Paul.

**Laura Ingalls Wilder** See page 80.

**August Wilson** See page 77.

**Steve Zahn (1967–)** is a TV and movie actor. His movies include *National Security* and *Daddy Day Care*. He also provided the voice of Runt in the animated film *Chicken Little*. He was born in Marshall.

Kirby Puckett

# RESOURCES

## BOOKS

### Nonfiction

Davis, Lucile. *The Mayo Brothers: Doctors to the World*. Danbury, Conn.: Children's Press, 1998.

Hasday, Judy L. *Minnesota*. Danbury, Conn.: Children's Press, 2003.

Kenney, Dave, Hillary Wackman, and Nancy O'Brien Wagner. *Northern Lights: The Stories of Minnesota's Past*. St. Paul: Minnesota Historical Society Press, 2003.

Marsh, Carole. *Minnesota History!: Surprising Secrets about Our State's Founding Mothers, Fathers & Kids!* Peachtree City, Ga.: Gallopade International, 1996.

Palazzo-Craig, Janet. *The Ojibwe of Michigan, Wisconsin, Minnesota, and North Dakota*. New York: PowerKids Press, 2005.

### Fiction

Brummer, Sandy. *Bound for Minnesota*. Anoka, Minn.: Expert Publishing, 2004.

Hoover, Helen. *Great Wolf and the Good Woodsman*. Minneapolis: University of Minnesota Press, 2005.

Mader, Patrick. *Oma Finds a Miracle*. Edina, Minn.: Beaver's Pond Press, 2007.

Paulsen, Gary. *The Winter Room*. New York: Orchard Books, 1999.

Rolvaag, Ole. *Giants in the Earth: A Saga of the Prairie*. New York: Harper, 1999.

Schultz, Jan Neubert. *Battle Cry*. Minneapolis: Carolrhoda Books, 2006.

Wargin, Kathy-jo. *The Legend of Minnesota*. Chelsea, Mich.: Sleeping Bear Press, 2006.

Wilder, Laura Ingalls. *On the Banks of Plum Creek*. New York: HarperTrophy, 2004.

# DVDs

*Minnesota (Discoveries . . . America).* Bennett-Watt Media, 2007.
*Paul Bunyan.* Schlessinger Media, 2006.
*The Saint Paul Winter Carnival (Great American Festivals).* HD Republic Productions, 2005.
*Voyageurs National Park, Minnesota.* Finley-Holiday, 2005.

# WEB SITES AND ORGANIZATIONS

### Explore Minnesota
*www.exploreminnesota.com*
To find out all the things to see and do in Minnesota.

### History of Minnesota
*www.mnsu.edu/emuseum/history/mnstatehistory*
To learn about each period in Minnesota's history, including lots of fun facts.

### Minnesota Author Biographies Project
*http://people.mnhs.org/authors/index.cfm*
To learn about dozens of Minnesota authors and their books.

### Minnesota Historical Society: Map of Historic Sites
*www.mnhs.org/places/sites*
For descriptions and photos of Minnesota's 26 state historic sites.

### Minnesota Secretary of State Student Page
*www.sos.state.mn.us/student/netscape4.html*
To learn about Minnesota's history, government, trivia, and much more.

### Minnesota State Parks
*www.dnr.state.mn.us/state_parks/index.html*
To find out about all the activities you can enjoy in Minnesota's state parks.

### Paul Bunyan Stories
*www.explorebrainerdlakes.com/visit/attract/paul/stories.htm*
To read some hilarious tales about the legendary lumberjack.

### State of Minnesota Home Page
*www.state.mn.us*
For information on state government, education, natural resources, and social services.

# INDEX

★ ★ ★

# AUTHOR'S TIPS AND SOURCE NOTES

★   ★   ★

As I did my research for this book, I especially enjoyed the Minnesota Historical Society's Web site (www.mnhs.org). There I found great first-person accounts in the letters and journals of early settlers, lumberjacks, and mill workers. The Tales of the Territory section (click on "Education") is full of fascinating historical information, too. Minnesota State University's EMuseum Web site (www.mnsu.edu/emuseum/index.shtml) provides a fantastic background on Minnesota's early civilizations, Native peoples, and immigrant cultures. You'll also find in-depth studies of the state's many immigrant groups in *They Chose Minnesota*, edited by June Holmquist. One pioneer, Alice Mendenhall George, gives a firsthand view of frontier life in *The Story of My Childhood, Written for My Children*. To see how Minnesota looked in the 1850s, try John Wesley Bond's *Minnesota and Its Resources*. The author's viewpoint is appropriate for its time, but he gives a good picture of Minnesota's natural landscape when it was still largely unsettled.